Lois Lowry

Twayne's United States Authors Series
Children's Literature

Ruth K. MacDonald, Editor

TUSAS 687

LOIS LOWRY

Lois Lowry

Joel D. Chaston

Southwest Missouri State University

Twayne Publishers
An Imprint of Simon & Schuster Macmillan
New York

Prentice Hall International
London • Mexico City • New Delhi • Singapore • Sydney • Toronto

Twayne's United States Authors Series No. 687

Lois Lowry
Joel D. Chaston

Twayne Publishers
An Imprint of Simon & Schuster Macmillan
1633 Broadway
New York, NY 10019

Library of Congress Cataloging-in-Publication Data

Chaston, Joel, 1954–
    Lois Lowry / Joel D. Chaston.
        p. cm. — (Twayne's United States authors series ; TUSAS 687)
    Includes bibliographical references and index.
    ISBN 0-8057-4034-1 (hard : alk. paper)
    1. Lowry, Lois—Criticism and interpretation. 2. Women and
literature—United States—History—20th century. 3. Young adult
fiction, American—History and criticism. 4. Children's stories,
American—History and criticism. I. Title. II. Series.
PS3562.0923Z64   1997
813'.54—dc21   97-8271
                                                                                                                CIP

10 9 8 7 6 5 4 3

Printed in the United States of America

For Rebecca, Chelsea, and Bradford

Contents

Preface

Lois Lowry's books are extremely popular with both young readers and adult critics. To date, Lowry has written 23 novels for children and young adults, works that include autobiographical, historical, humorous, and problem fiction. She has won almost every major award given for American children's books, including the *Boston Globe-Horn Book* Award for fiction (*Rabble Starkey*), the Golden Kite Award from the Society of Children's Book Writers (*Rabble Starkey*), the International Reading Association Children's Book Award (*A Summer to Die*), the Newbery Prize (*Number the Stars* and *The Giver*), and the Regina Medal (*The Giver*). At the same time, her 12 books about the Krupnik family and three about Caroline and J. P. Tate have ensured her continued popularity with young readers. Several of Lowry's works have appeared on lists of best-selling children's books, and her works frequently dominate children's choice awards in many states.

At the moment there has been no comprehensive critical study of Lowry's work, although *Number the Stars* and *The Giver* have engendered many scholarly and pedagogical articles. Lowry, who is clearly one of the most important twentieth-century American writers for children, certainly deserves closer critical attention. In this book I provide a careful reading and an aesthetic critique of the themes, style, and structure of her books, relating them to each other and to works by other writers.

My first chapter discusses Lowry's life and the events, books, and ideas that have influenced her work and shaped her as a writer. Chapter 2 examines Lowry's three early novels for children and young adults: *A Summer to Die; Find a Stranger, Say Goodbye;* and *Autumn Street*. These novels grapple with the nature of her audience and establish Lowry as an important voice among writers for the young. The sometimes serious tone and topics of these books, which include death and loss, serve as a sharp contrast to much of Lowry's later humorous work.

Chapters 3 and 4 delve into the 12 books that feature Anastasia and Sam Krupnik as protagonists. Although these works have been acclaimed by reviewers, they have received little serious consideration, perhaps because they are humorous and episodic. Read as a whole, however, the Anastasia books are a unified study of the development of the imagination and the growth of a young girl through adolescence, whereas the Sam stories explore the early years of a child's development. I also explore connections between the Anastasia books and earlier works of children's literature, as well as Lowry's use of humor, which, as Eric Kimmel has suggested, is closely related to tragedy.

Chapter 5 deals with works that are perhaps less complex than many of Lowry's other novels. These books and short stories, including three about Caroline and J. P. Tate, are extremely popular and have won several young reader awards. Many of these works deal with children from nontraditional or dysfunctional families who are searching for their identities, often in "green places." They also investigate themes common to Lowry's other work and, in the context of other humorous children's books, reveal Lowry's comic genius.

Chapter 6 treats Lowry's three most critically acclaimed works: *Rabble Starkey*, *Number the Stars*, and *The Giver*, each of which demonstrates Lowry's ability to stretch and experiment while tackling serious subjects such as the nature of true friendship, bravery, and the value of individual freedom. These are works that will ensure Lowry's literary reputation and readership for years to come. Chapter 7 explores both Lowry's achievement as a writer and her impact on contemporary children's fiction.

In completing this study, I would like to thank Lois Lowry herself, who generously allowed me to visit her home in Cambridge, Massachusetts, where I spent a day interviewing her. She has furnished additional information in telephone conversations and letters and provided me with the photograph for the cover and frontispiece. I am indebted to Lowry for much of the biographical information in this book, as well as the many novels she has written, which have made writing this book a pleasure.

I must also thank Karen Hoyle and the staff of the University of Minnesota Children's Literature Research Library for their hospitality and help while researching Lowry's manuscripts in the Kerlan Collection. I am especially grateful for Karen Hoyle's help in seeing that her library had acquired the manuscripts for *Number the Stars* and *The Giver* before my visit. My appreciation also goes to Southwest Missouri State University, which provided me with two grants, making possible my travel to interview Lowry and to visit the Kerlan Collection, as well as the time to work on this project.

I am grateful to my colleagues at Southwest Missouri State University, especially Phyllis Bixler, who gave me feedback on my manuscript, and Judith John and Linda Benson, who encouraged me along the way. Finally, I am indebted to my wife, Rebecca, and my children, Chelsea and Bradford, who, as always, have given me their support.

Chronology

1937   Lois Hammersberg Lowry born March 20 in Honolulu, Hawaii, to Robert E. Hammersberg and Katharine Landis.

1939   Moves to Brooklyn, New York.

1942   Moves to Carlisle, Pennsylvania, to live with her grandfather while her father is overseas.

1943   Brother, Jon, born. Attends first through sixth grade in Carlisle, skipping second because she is an advanced reader.

1948   Moves to Tokyo, Japan, where she attends seventh and eighth grade.

1950   Moves back to Carlisle, Pennsylvania, where she begins ninth grade.

1951   Moves to Governors Island off the tip of Manhattan. Attends Curtis High School on Staten Island.

1952   Attends Packer Collegiate Institute in Brooklyn Heights during her last two years of high school.

1954   Enters Pembroke College, the women's branch of Brown University.

1956   Marries Donald Grey Lowry, a naval officer, June 11. Moves to San Diego, California.

1958   Moves to New London, Connecticut. Daughter Alix born.

1959   Moves to Key West, Florida. Son Grey born.

1960   Moves to Charleston, South Carolina.

1961   Moves to Cambridge, Massachusetts. Daughter Kristin born.

1962   Son Benjamin born. Lowry's sister, Helen, dies.

1963   Moves to Portland, Maine.

1972   Receives B.A. from University of Southern Maine.

1973   *Black American Literature* (textbook edited by Lowry).

1974 *Literature of the American Revolution* (textbook edited by Lowry). Begins publishing articles in magazines and newspapers such as the *New York Times*, *Down East*, and *Yankee*. Also works as a freelance photographer.

1975 "Crow Call" published in *Redbook*.

1977 *A Summer to Die*. "The Recital" published in *Philadelphia*. Divorces Donald Grey Lowry. Moves to Cape Porpoise, Maine.

1978 *Here at Kennebunkport* and *Find a Stranger, Say Good-Bye*. Receives International Reading Association Children's Book Award for *A Summer to Die*.

1979 *Anastasia Krupnik*. Moves to Boston, Massachusetts.

1980 *Autumn Street*. Begins living with Martin Small.

1981 *Anastasia Again!*

1982 *Anastasia at Your Service*.

1983 *The One Hundredth Thing about Caroline* and *Taking Care of Terrific*. Divides time between Boston and a newly purchased farmhouse in New Hampshire.

1984 *Anastasia Ask Your Analyst* and *Us and Uncle Fraud*.

1985 *Anastasia on Her Own* and *Switcharound*.

1986 *Anastasia Has the Answers*.

1987 *Anastasia's Chosen Career* and *Rabble Starkey*. Receives Golden Kite Award and *Boston Globe-Horn Book* Award for Fiction for *Rabble Starkey*.

1988 *All about Sam*.

1989 *Number the Stars*. Receives Sydney Taylor Award for *Number the Stars*.

1990 *Your Move, J. P.* Receives John Newbery Medal and National Jewish Book Award for *Number the Stars*.

1991 *Anastasia at This Address*.

1992 *Attaboy, Sam!*

1993 *The Giver*. Moves to Cambridge, Massachusetts.

1994 Receives John Newbery Medal, the Regina Medal, and a *Boston Globe-Horn Book* Honor for *The Giver*.

1995   *Anastasia, Absolutely*. Lowry's son Grey is killed in a plane crash.

1996   *See You Around, Sam!* Receives honorary doctorate from University of Southern Maine.

1997   *Stay!: Keeper's Tale*.

Chapter One

The Inward Eye

Visiting a literature class that her father teaches at Harvard University, 10-year-old Anastasia in Lois Lowry's *Anastasia Krupnik* (1979) finds the experience boring, except for a poem the students discuss, William Wordsworth's "I Wandered Lonely as a Cloud." Anastasia especially likes Wordsworth's phrase "the inward eye," which means "memory" and which is "the bliss of solitude."[1] Anastasia, who wants to become a writer, is concerned, however, because she has no powerful memories of her own from which to draw. Toward the end of the novel, after her grandmother dies, Anastasia decides that she now has acquired some significant memories and has "an inward eye for the first time" (*Anastasia,* 100).

Lowry's books are replete with characters who, like Anastasia, are either trying to develop their "inward eye" or who are gaining self-knowledge through using it. For example, Natalie Armstrong in *Find a Stranger, Say Goodbye* (1978) thinks she needs the memories of her biological mother to gain an identity; Elizabeth Lorimer of *Autumn Street* (1980) mentally paints memories of her childhood in the novel's opening chapter; and Jonas of *The Giver* (1993) risks his life to return memories to an entire society that has lost them.

Sitting in the basement office of her home in Cambridge, Massachusetts, one October morning in 1994, Lois Lowry talked about the importance of memory in her work. "Clearly, that's an obsession of mine," she laughed, "and something that permeates my writing and therefore permeates my thought. . . . I believe I have had what is called an eidetic memory, which is sort of photographic in its nature, so that . . . when I remember something, I see it." As a result, Lowry believes that in writing about children she relives her own childhood. "I go back in a subjective way and look out through my eyes at eight or ten or thirteen," she says, "but also refeel the emotions that child felt seeing those experiences."[2]

Lowry is a fine storyteller whose memories often provoke laughter. Inspired by photographs during the interview, Lowry occasionally launched into a story, as when she spoke of her glamorous older sister,

Helen, who died of cancer in her twenties, or her grandparents' home in Carlisle, Pennsylvania, where she lived during World War II. The two Newbery Medals Lowry has won reminded her that another children's writer, Russell Freedman, suggested that she use them as matching earrings. As time passed, it became increasingly clear that Lowry's books have also been greatly affected by her own life and memories. Some of her works are partly autobiographical, such as *A Summer to Die* (1977) and *Autumn Street*, whereas another, *Number the Stars* (1989), was inspired by the reminiscences of a good friend. Even her fantastic, dystopian novel, *The Giver* (1993), grew out of some important personal memories. As a result, Lowry's own life provides important insight into the many critically acclaimed children's books she has created.

Early Childhood

Lowry's father, Robert Hammersberg, grew up in Wisconsin, where his relatives had settled after immigrating from Norway. Because their original family name, Anderson, was so common among the Scandinavian immigrants working on the railroad, it was changed to Hammersberg after the family's hometown in Norway. Robert's father, Carl Hammersberg, had died while Robert was young, but his mother, Cena, lived long enough to become an important part of Lowry's childhood.[3]

After graduating from dental school at Marquette University in Wisconsin, Robert Hammersberg was commissioned in the Army Dental Corps. Eventually he would become chief of dental services at Walter Reed Hospital and numbered Douglas MacArthur and Richard Nixon among his patients. While Robert was stationed at Carlisle Barracks in Pennsylvania, he met Katharine Landis, who had lived in Carlisle all of her life. She would become Lowry's mother.

Lowry's great-grandfather Landis had left the Amish farm where he grew up to get an education, and her grandfather was a very distinguished bank president. Lowry recalls that he was once mentioned in a question on the television game show *Jeopardy:* "The question was, 'Bank president Merkel Landis founded this in Pennsylvania.' The answer was: 'The Christmas Club.' "[4] Lowry's maternal grandmother, Helen Boyd, was one of four sisters, all college graduates, as Lowry notes, an unusual achievement at the turn of the century. Lowry's own mother became a kindergarten teacher before getting married.

In 1933, Robert Hammersberg and Katharine Landis were married at Fort Benning, Georgia, where Lowry's older sister, Helen Boyd, named after her maternal grandmother, was born the following year. Three years later, on March 20, 1937, while her father was stationed at Schofield Barracks on Oahu, Lowry was born. Initially, she had been named "Cena" after her fraternal grandmother, who, however, felt that no one should be burdened with such a name. As a result, at the age of 11 months, she was christened "Lois Ann" after her father's two sisters back in Wisconsin.

When she was two years old, Lowry's father was transferred from Hawaii to New York, and the family moved to Brooklyn. Describing the boat ride when she left Hawaii, Lowry writes that, according to her mother, she whimpered about the cold and wanted to go home: "It must have been hard to explain to a shivering two-year-old that 'home' was not a permanent thing."[5] Lowry's memories of Brooklyn include a visit to the 1940 World's Fair in New York with her family and her first experiences reading, although she cannot recall the actual process of learning to read. One day her mother was quite astonished to learn that her three-year-old had this ability. According to Lowry's mother, a professor from the education department of Dickinson College came to observe this child prodigy, and young Lois read aloud to him an article from the *Saturday Evening Post* to demonstrate her abilities (Chaston 1994).

Lowry's precociousness was evident even in nursery school, where she disliked most of the games and activities, especially marching around the room like an elephant, and preferred sitting in a corner and reading. Lowry distinctly remembers hearing the 1941 radio broadcast announcing the bombing of Pearl Harbor, an event that she would later incorporate into her novel *Autumn Street*. The bombing meant that, as a career army officer, Lowry's father would soon be transferred to the Pacific.

Carlisle, Pennsylvania

In 1942, with her husband involved in the war, Katharine Hammersberg, who was pregnant again, took her children to live in Carlisle, Pennsylvania, with her father, who had remarried after her mother passed away. Lowry adored her grandfather but disliked her stepgrandmother, who was not used to children. In January of 1943, just before Lowry's sixth birthday, her brother, Jon, was born. Lowry and her siblings would be deprived of their father's presence—due to his military career—during much of her childhood. "I remember all these relatively normal Christmases," Lowry explains, "except that they had this enormous hole in them because there was never any father. . . . That's probably why I've written a terrific father figure into almost all of my books." (Miller, 130). Lowry's mother, on the other hand, like many women of her day, was very much present, having quit working when she married so she would be able to take care of her children.

Lowry began first grade in Carlisle, walking the few blocks to Franklin School, which she attended through sixth grade. In first grade, Lowry, who could read "real" books, was bored with basal readers. Toward the end of the year, Lowry's first-grade teacher—taking advantage of her pupil's ability—told the rest of the class to "go ask Lois" for help if they were unable to decipher a word. When the class read a story about raising chickens, Lowry recalls, the other students, one by one, came to her desk for help with the word "incubator" (Chaston 1994).

An advanced reader, Lowry skipped from first to third grade, which she liked, except for the multiplication tables. From then on, she was usually the youngest and smallest in her school classes and the one who suffered from math anxiety. Furthermore, Lowry was by nature a shy child; she explains, "I liked nothing better than to curl up with a book." In later years, with her family on the move and continually facing the necessity of making new friends, she explains that reading "was my comforting life that I took with me again and again. . . . It was a kind of retreat that I read a lot and it served me well" (Chaston 1994).

Childhood Reading and Writing

At home, Lowry's family continued to encourage her interest in reading. Her mother had read aloud to her children when they were young, and Lowry discovered books like Margaret Sidney's *Five Little Peppers and How They Grew* (1881) and Charles Kingsley's *The Water Babies* (1863) in her grandfather's vast library. In "The Recital," an autobiographical story in *Philadelphia*, Lowry describes how her grandfather introduced her to poetry: "It was the little girl's grandfather, each night, who put her to bed. He was a man whose tastes ran to authenticated antiques and 19th-century literature, both properly polished. So each night he lifted her, in her pajamas, into a mahogany four poster bed and read to her from a leatherbound volume of poetry. His favorite poem was 'Thanatopsis' by William Cullen Bryant."[6]

This same piece also recounts how Lowry quickly memorized the fairly lengthy 'Thanatopsis' to the amazement of one of her grandfather's friends, Judge Biddle, an old bachelor who adored Lois and read her highbrow poetry. As Lowry related in an interview in *Contemporary Authors*, "[E]very year for years after that he [Judge Biddle] gave me a book of poetry on my birthday. Even after I moved away, this book would come every year in the mail, Tennyson or Longfellow."[7] Some years later, when Biddle died, he left Lowry one-half of 1 percent of his estate in his will, hoping that she would use it for graduate school. Lowry guiltily recollects that instead she used it to buy a pale blue Pontiac, which made her the envy of her college friends.

The young Lowry devoured books more or less indiscriminately. She loved not only series books such as those about the Bobbsey twins and Nancy Drew but also comics such as *Captain Marvel* and *Little Lulu*. Every month 11-year-old Lois would pay 10 cents for the latest edition of *Little Lulu*. "I can remember thinking," she says, "as I held my *Little Lulu* comic book, 'I'm going to grow up and I'm going to become an adult and I'll change in many ways, but I'll never outgrow my love of *Little Lulu*' " (Chaston 1994).

For Lowry, the public library was a special place. Visiting there alone, she read through the entire children's section and then began on the adult books. She fondly recalls P. L. Travers's *Mary Poppins* (1934) and John Steinbeck's *The Red Pony* (1937), which figures prominently in the plot of her own novel *Rabble Starkey* (1987). Lowry wanted to grow up to be a writer like Lois Lenski, author of another beloved book, *Indian Captive* (1941).[8] In an introduction to *Dear Author: Students Write about the Books That Changed Their Lives* (1995), Lowry includes a letter she imagines she would have sent Lenski when she was younger. She writes that sometimes she thinks of herself as "Corn-Tassel," the nickname Lenski's heroine received from her captors. Lowry also includes an imaginary letter to Harper Lee. "I became Scout when I read [*To Kill a Mockingbird* (1960)]," she writes, "and have been Scout ever since."[9] In the same essay, Lowry talks of other writers who influenced her: Gustave Flaubert, when Lowry was 15 and felt that her "life was as dull and unrewarding as Emma Bovary's"; J. D. Salinger, when she was 16; and Thomas Hardy the following year (*Author*, x).

Like her own heroine Anastasia Krupnik, Lowry also relished deathbed scenes and tales of orphaned or crippled children, as in Louisa May Alcott's *Little Women* (1868) and Francis Hodgson Burnett's *Secret Garden* (1911). In an afterword to a 1986 edition of Eleanor H. Porter's *Pollyanna* (1913), Lowry describes how, at the age of eight or nine, she reveled in that story, yearning to be a poor orphan who is "[m]istreated, misunderstood; an innocent (young, blond) victim, set upon by fate and misfortune. And then to top it off: *crippled*."[10] As a more cynical 13-year-old, however, she suddenly found *Pollyanna* disgusting and set it aside to pursue Margaret Mitchell's romantic novel, *Gone with the Wind* (1936).

The childhood books that Lowry mentions most frequently, however, are Marjorie Kinnan Rawlings's *The Yearling* (1946) and Betty Smith's *A Tree Grows in Brooklyn* (1943), which she cannot recollect "without getting all choked up."[11] "The [books] I remember, still with a chill up my back because they were so wonderful, are the ones with scenes that just whacked me over the head," Lowry reminisces. When Lowry was 9 and her sister 12, their mother had discovered *The Yearling*, a Book-of-the-Month-Club selection, and read it to them. "I can only guess," Lowry recounts, "that she herself was so affected by it that she wanted to share it with us" (Chaston 1994). At age 10, Lowry checked out *A Tree Grows in Brooklyn* from the local library, to the chagrin of the librarian, who warned her mother that the book was not for children. For Lowry, these two books inspired melodramatic fantasies, much like those that grew out of *Pollyanna*. "Combining both books," she writes, "I have two not-exactly-compatible dreams. I yearn to live in teeming slums, and to forge a life for myself amid the dangers of poverty-stricken streets. If that isn't possible . . . my second choice is to live in a swamp and have mostly animals for friends: animals, and one poor little crippled boy, who would die young so that I could weep at his graveside" ("Lois Lowry," 138).

Like Elizabeth in the autobiographical *Autumn Street*, Lowry was also a good artist. When Lowry was 10, her teacher, Mrs. O'Hara, asked her to draw the hardest part of the classroom mural of a wagon train—the oxen—a task she dutifully performed but resented because it was not as exciting as other parts of the project.[12] Years later, although realizing that her true talent lay in writing, Lowry temporarily contemplated studying art at college.

During her years in Carlisle, Lowry's writer's imagination was clearly developing. Once she broke a doll that belonged to an aunt, obliging her mother to make a trip to New York to get it fixed. Lowry fantasized that her mother was bringing home a real baby sister instead of a doll. After being disappointed, she turned the experience into a story for herself. "Unaware," Lowry writes, "I [was] beginning to be a writer" ("Lois Lowry," 137). On another occasion, Lowry was so fascinated by her mother's tale of three Carlisle children who had been killed that she went to the local historical society to research the event.

In August of 1947, 10-year-old Lowry saw her name in print for the first time. Like many other children, she had written a letter to *Jack and*

Jill, a magazine to which her mother had bought her a subscription. At the time, Lowry was attending a summer camp, and, because the camp counselors seemed more interested in children with college-age brothers, she had created a fictional brother, "David," who was attending Princeton. When her mother sent her a copy of the magazine that featured her letter, Lowry had to hide it from her campmates because it included a description of her family that made it clear that there was no David (Chaston 1994).

In an autobiographical sketch, Lowry writes about some of the joys of this period in her life: learning to ride a bicycle on the brick sidewalks bordering Dickinson College and attending cowboy movies on Saturday afternoons ("Lois Lowry," 137). Sunday mornings, she sat restless and irritable through meetings at the local Presbyterian church, but in the evenings her grandparents would take her to outdoor concerts at Dickinson College.[13] Summers were often spent at her grandparents' lakeside home, a massive, converted nineteenth-century mill located about 15 miles from Carlisle.

Japan

Although World War II ended when Lowry was eight, her father had stayed on in Japan as part of the occupation forces. In 1948, Lowry and her family joined him after a summer during which she had suffered through the inoculations required for traveling abroad. While in Japan, the Hammersbergs lived in Tokyo, although Lowry would travel to the island of Eta Jima to visit a friend from school whose father had transferred there. In her Newbery acceptance speech for *The Giver* (1993), Lowry describes living in Japan: "We live there, in the center of that huge Japanese city, in a small American enclave with a very American name: Washington Heights. We live in an American-style house, with American neighbors, and our little community has its own movie theater, which shows American movies, and a small church, a tiny library, and an elementary school; and in many ways it is an odd replica of a United States village."[14] Lowry, however, enjoyed exploring the non-Americanized sections of the city and would ride her bicycle to the Shibuya district. She recalls that the Japanese were both kind and curious and that they seemed to love children, especially American blondes.

While in Tokyo, Lowry and her sister attended Meguro, an English-speaking school where most of her classmates were also children of military personnel. As when she was younger, Lois liked the academic

aspects of school but not the group activities: "[S]omehow, the instant I
am told that I have to memorize rules, recite a pledge, earn a badge, or
turn a cartwheel in unison with other cartwheel turners—well, somehow, it all begins to seem like that dumb elephant-marching game the
kids had played back in nursery school. I prefer to be on my own, and
usually manage to be" ("Lois Lowry," 139).

High School and College

In 1950, with the beginning of the Korean War, American women and
children were evacuated from Japan, and Lowry's mother again took her
children to Carlisle, Pennsylvania, where Lois attended ninth and the
first part of 10th grade. At that point, her father returned to the United
States and was transferred to New York, where the family lived on Governors Island, off the tip of Manhattan. Initially, Lowry attended Curtis
High School on Staten Island, which required two different ferryboat
rides to get there. Eventually Lowry, lonely and somewhat intimidated
by the other students, convinced her parents to send her to a private
high school. As a result, Lowry commuted to the Packer Collegiate
Institute in Brooklyn Heights for her junior and senior years and graduated in a class of 46 students. Lowry enjoyed English classes, detested
gym, and was a good student. The caption under her picture in her
senior yearbook reads, "Future Novelist."

In high school, despite encouragement from guidance counselors and
teachers, Lowry was not much of a "joiner." For the first time, however,
she felt that her teachers took a real interest in their students. When she
was a junior, she wrote a poem for English class that her teacher submitted to a competition for high school writers. It won and was subsequently published. Lowry also recalls that her Latin teacher took her to
see her first opera (Chaston 1994).

In the fall of 1954, Lowry enrolled in Pembroke College, the
women's branch of Brown University. Although Brown had a good
writing program and Lowry had dreams of becoming a writer, she
enrolled there primarily because she was offered a scholarship. According to Lowry, she lived in a small dormitory, "a converted private home,
with a group of perhaps fourteen other girls. We are very much alike.
We wear the same sort of clothes: cashmere sweaters and plaid wool
skirts, knee socks and loafers. We all smoke Marlboro cigarettes, and we
knit—usually argyle socks for our boyfriends—and play bridge. Sometimes we study; and we get good grades because we are all the cream of

the crop, the valedictorians and class presidents from our high schools all over the United States" ("Newbery 1994," 416).

Working hard at becoming a writer, Lowry met with one of her professors as part of a special honors program for aspiring writers. Although praising her "fluency" and impeccable grammar, he told her that, based on her stories about small children whose dogs die, she had evidently not experienced much of life yet. Lowry suggests, tongue in cheek, that she was "a great success at college of the 1950s" ("Lois Lowry," 140). She had dates every Saturday night and soon had a fraternity pin on her sweater, followed by a diamond ring on her finger. Lowry was married at the end of her sophomore year, shortly after her 19th birthday. Her husband was 21.

Marriage

On June 11, 1956, Lois Ann Hammersberg married Donald Grey Lowry, then a newly commissioned naval officer, and she left school to travel with him to San Diego, where he was stationed. From there the Lowrys moved to New London, Connecticut, where their first daughter, Alix, was born in 1958. When the family relocated to Key West, Florida, a year later, Lowry's first son, Grey, was born. After a year in Charleston, South Carolina, Lowry's husband left the military to attend Harvard Law School, and the family settled in an apartment in Cambridge, Massachusetts. In order to help with finances, Lowry worked for a time at the Harvard Coop, a university bookstore, and also did some typing for a professor. In 1961 Lowry's second daughter, Kristin, was born and was followed a year later by another son, Benjamin.

In 1963, Lowry's family moved to Portland, Maine, so that her husband could begin his law practice. Lowry remarks that both she and her children grew up in Maine. For a while, when her children were small, she did a lot of what she calls "elephant-marching," participating in "committees and boards and probably even a Tupperware party or two" before retreating to her own corner to read as she had ever since nursery school ("Lois Lowry," 141). Lowry describes her family life at this time as fairly ordinary. "It was a very typical marriage. We had a nice house and a horse in the back pasture and a big dog and a station wagon. It's almost cliché-ridden. Our Christmas cards always had four blonde kids and a big dog. It was a nice, pleasant interlude" (Chaston 1994).

During these years in Maine, Lowry pursued her interests in both literature and writing. After her son Benjamin started school, Lowry went back to college. Four years later, in 1972, she graduated with a B.A. in English literature from the University of Southern Maine. She then began graduate studies there, completed her coursework for a master's degree in English, and began working on her thesis. By then Lowry had developed a successful career as a freelance journalist. She told herself, "You don't need this degree to do what you really want to do and people are paying you to write these things and no one's going to . . . care about this boring thesis you're writing, so I didn't finish—which I sort of regret only because I can't say that I have a master's degree" (Chaston 1994). In 1996 Lowry finally received her graduate degree in the form of an honorary doctorate from her alma mater.

Photography and Freelance Writing

In graduate school Lowry discovered that she could receive credit by taking a photography class that sounded interesting. "It turned out not to be as much fun as it was work," Lowry told an interviewer. "But I discovered that I enjoyed it and that I was good at it, so I began on the side doing photographs professionally, both for a textbook company that needed a lot of work done and privately, specializing in children's portraits" (Ross, 335). For a number of years, she traveled around New England taking pictures of children. Her expertise as a child photographer is evident from a 1975 feature article she wrote for the *New York Times*, "Picturing Children as They Really Are." Years later, a portrait she took of a young Swedish girl would serve as the cover of Lowry's *Number the Stars* (1990). As her career as a freelance journalist developed, Lowry also took pictures to accompany her articles. Eventually she was asked to produce a collection of photographs of houses and buildings in Kennebunkport, Maine, which became *Here at Kennebunkport* (1978).

While in graduate school, Lowry also published her first two books, high school literature texts, projects that gave her independent study credits in her graduate program. She had become acquainted with a textbook publisher who was looking for someone to write a textbook about African-American literature. Although Lowry felt that the job should have gone to an African-American, she took the job because nobody else was offering her book contracts. This first book became *Black American Literature* (1973); it was followed by *Literature of the American Revolution*, a bicentennial book (1974).

Lowry's first freelance magazine article, which she notes "would hardly go down as great literature," was the result of teaching a six-week course in poetry writing for children at Trinity Episcopal Church, where the family attended services (Chaston 1994). Lowry invited a photographer friend to come in and take photographs of the children writing, and she subsequently published an article about the experience in *The Episcopalian*.

From 1974 through 1979, Lowry produced a variety of articles, often travel pieces such as "Eastport Maine: The Same Salty Whiff" (*Yankee* 1975) and "The Colonial Life at Strawberry Banke" (*New York Times* 1976) as well as biographical feature articles such as "The Maine Boy-hoods of Longfellow and Hawthorne" (*Down East* 1976) and "King of the Occult" (*Down East* 1977), about another Maine writer, Stephen King, who was gaining popularity. Lowry was a regular contributor to *Down East* and wrote articles for them almost on a monthly basis. She also published frequently in the Sunday *New York Times*. One of her favorite articles for the *Times*, "How Does It Feel to be on a TV Quiz Show? Don't Ask" (1974), describes her experience as a contestant on the television quiz show *Jeopardy*, hosted at that time by Art Fleming. Goaded on by her children, who thought she knew more than the contestants on the program, Lowry took a qualifying test and was accepted. As a contestant, she tried to follow the advice of the producers and their assistants and was careful not to argue with the host, who erroneously introduced her as the author of a history book. The climax of this humorous essay is Lowry's defeat due to missing a final question about Whitey Ford, one that her 14-year-old son could have answered. In the end, Lowry took the $400 she won, along with the consolation prize—a *Jeopardy* board game—and trudged out of the studio, symbolically pressing "the NBC elevator button DOWN."[15] Such an experience might very easily have happened to her later literary creation, Anastasia Krupnik.

One of the interviews Lowry conducted for a magazine article would greatly affect her later work. She was sent to write an article about a painter who lived alone on an island off the coast of Maine. She writes, "I spend a good deal of time with this man, and we talk a lot about color. It is clear to me that although I am a highly visual person—a person who sees and appreciates form and composition and color—this man's capacity for seeing color goes far beyond mine" ("Newbery 1994," 17). Although the article was never published, the artist she interviewed, Carl Nelson, has appeared in Lowry's novels in various guises. According to a 1985 videotape interview for Houghton Mifflin, Nelson was the inspiration for Will Banks in *A Summer to Die*, as well as for Tallie, Natalie's artist-grandmother, who also lives on an island, in

Find a Stranger, Say Goodbye.[16] In her "Newbery Acceptance" for *The Giver*, Lowry now relates that she subconsciously had Nelson in mind when creating the novel's title character and eventually chose a photograph she had taken of him for the cover.

An interviewer for the *Los Angeles Times* describes Lowry's early attempts at writing as "the dilettante journalist career that the wife of a successful lawyer can afford to pursue. She wrote a free-lance magazine article here, an occasional short story there. Sooner or later, she figured, she'd settle down and produce the great American novel—for grown-ups, of course."[17]

Becoming a Children's Writer

It was during her last years in Maine that Lowry finally began her career as a children's writer. When her children were young, she had written stories for them such as "Caroline Cauliflower" and "The Hippo in the Hollyhocks," a self-illustrated story. In two published short stories of this period, "The Recital" and "Crow Call" (1975), Lowry turned to her own childhood experiences for material. "Crow Call," a short autobiographical piece in which a young girl and her father go hunting for crows, brought Lowry to the attention of Melanie Kroupa, then an editor at Houghton Mifflin. Unbeknownst to Lowry, Walter Lorraine, head of Houghton Mifflin's children's book department, had asked his editors to read magazines in search of potential children's writers. As part of this strategy, Kroupa wrote to Lowry asking if she had ever considered writing for children. "I felt very flattered and singled out," Lowry recalls. "I didn't know that they were writing to every author who could put two sentences together. Walter did tell me later that of all these authors that they wrote to, I was the only one that they ever gave a book contract" (Chaston 1994). The result of the contract was *A Summer to Die* (1977), which drew on Lowry's relationship with her sister, Helen. "The emotions of the younger sister were accurate to my own life experience," Lowry admits. "I changed all of the details, except the personalities" (Chaston 1994). In the opening scene of the novel, based on a real-life event, the older sibling, Molly, draws a line down the center of the bedroom she shares with her sister.

As a teenager, Lowry had thought that her sister was "the most glamorous thing that ever lived," a notion supported by a photograph of her sister taken when Helen was a nominee for homecoming queen at Pennsylvania State (Chaston 1994). Helen was married the same week she graduated from college, and her husband, like Lowry's, was also in the military. She had subsequently moved to Germany and then Texas, giving birth to three children. A few weeks after Lowry gave birth to her second son, Benjamin, Helen died of cancer at a Washington, D.C., hospital. Because of her own pregnancy, Lowry had not been permitted to visit her sister before she died. Since *A Summer to Die* was intended for a middle-grade audience, Lowry had to change the ages of the two sisters.

Lowry did not show her potential publishers the manuscript of *A Summer to Die* until it was completed: "I lived in Maine and I just wrote it and when I was finished sent it to them. And they decided to publish it" (Chaston 1994). As a result, Lowry has never undergone the arduous process of submitting her book manuscripts to publisher after publisher and has never received a rejection letter. From that point on, Houghton Mifflin became the publisher for all of her books. When *A Summer to Die* became a success, it was named to the *Horn Book* Honor List and won the 1978 International Reading Association Award, given to new children's writers who show outstanding promise. According to a 1994 article in the *Los Angeles Times*, the novel has been translated into nine languages and has sold more than 45,000 hardcover copies.

In 1977, Lowry and her husband divorced. "When I was nineteen," she writes, "I had pretended to be—maybe I actually was—someone who cared a lot about bedmaking and rulemaking and homemaking. Later, after I grew up, I turned out to be somebody else entirely. Fortunately my kids liked me anyway—of course they didn't have many options" ("Lois Lowry," 142). In an interview with Mickey Pearlman, Lowry explains that her husband "didn't want to be married to somebody who now said she was a writer and was going to go off and do stuff and earn money."[18] In the same interview, she describes a telling incident. When she had started writing seriously, Lowry had put a small table in the corner of her husband's study (a room he required, although he rarely worked at home). On the table, Lowry kept an electric typewriter her father had bought for her. In retrospect, she pictures herself "as a little mouse sitting in the corner of a room in which everything belonged to someone else, except that corner." One day, Lowry came back from a magazine assignment and found her typewriter was missing. Her husband had lent it to someone in her absence. "He didn't perceive," Lowry says, "and I think still wouldn't perceive, what a dagger to my heart that was" (Pearlman, 175).

Lowry stayed on in Maine for two more years after her divorce, moving from a 12-room house in the country to a three-room apartment over a garage. "I had a romantic vision," Lowry confesses, "that a writer should live in a small, coastal, bleak town—and so I moved to a place called Cape Porpoise, Maine. Summer was nice, but winter was the pits."[19]

In 1978, Lowry published her second novel, *Find a Stranger, Say Goodbye*. Her editor for *A Summer to Die* went on to work for another publisher, but Lowry stayed with Houghton Mifflin, working directly with Walter Lorraine, who took her on and became the primary editor for all her books. Like *A Summer to Die*, *Find a Stranger, Say Goodbye* focuses on a young adult trying to define her place in her family. In this case, Natalie Armstrong, who is part of a strong, supportive family, embarks on a search for her biological mother. *A Summer to Die* had dealt with Lowry's own experience, so she was "casting about for something else to base a book on" (Chaston 1994). Her own children were still fairly young and she had friends who were still having babies. Some of them were unable to have children and had opted for adoption. At that same time, another friend, "a woman in her thirties, married with children," who had been adopted when she was five months old, received a letter from a female college professor "who introduced herself as her . . . birth mother and wanted to get together" (Chaston 1994).

In the novel, Natalie's search takes her from her small town in Maine, up the New England coast, and then to New York City, where she meets her biological mother before returning to her own family. Reviewers treated the book as one of a number of problem novels published at the time, suggesting that its "melodrama and sweetness will appeal to young teens who yearn for a comfortable amalgam of the romanticism of the 40s and 50s and the new realism of the 70s."[20] In 1980, the novel was adapted as an episode of *NBC Special Treats* called "I Don't Know Who I Am," a production that was nominated for an Emmy Award even though Lowry herself does not particularly care for the program.

That same year, Lowry left Maine. With the exception of her youngest son, her children were all on their own, and, having been single for two years, Lowry felt isolated and decided to move to Boston. Contemplating relocating to San Francisco, she had visited friends there but opted ultimately for Boston. Lowry recalls that she picked up a *Boston Globe*, looked for an apartment, and said, "Fine, I'll take it." "It was very haphazard," Lowry says, "how it worked out so well" (Chaston 1994). Soon after relocating to Boston, Lowry, who mistakenly thought she would be able to drive a car in that big city, went looking for automobile insurance. As a result of her search she met Martin Small, an insurance agency executive with whom she has lived "very happily since 1980" ("Lois Lowry," 143).

In 1979, *Anastasia Krupnik*, the first of many books about Anastasia and her family, appeared. The book began as a short story that Lowry wrote as comic relief while working on another novel, the much more serious *Autumn Street*. Having become fond of the title character, Lowry decided to expand the story instead of submitting it to a children's magazine.

"My first two books had been serious and I was determined to do something in a lighter vein," Lowry explains. "This was when Jimmy Carter was in the White House and his daughter, Amy, was always getting into trouble—which of course she continued to do for many years. But still, I get a kick out of her. There's a lot of Amy in Anastasia."[21] Anastasia is also "a composite of [her] two quite nutty daughters" (Ross, 334). For example, Lowry's daughter Kristin once answered some of her mother's fan mail, much like Anastasia does in *Anastasia Again!* (1981) ("Visit"). At the time Lowry had not intended to turn the book into a series, underestimating Anastasia's potential appeal to her readers. *Anastasia Krupnik* was named an American Library Association Notable Book and was favorably reviewed. The book is popular with children and teachers, who particularly enjoy Anastasia's experiences writing poetry for her very nonpoetic fourth-grade teacher, Mrs. Westvessel. Excerpts from the book have been anthologized in collections such as Judith Saltman's college textbook, *The Riverside Anthology of Children's Literature* (sixth edition, 1985).[22]

In 1980 Lowry published *Autumn Street*, which draws heavily on her early years in Pennsylvania. "The book, *Autumn Street*, is one of my favorites because it comes from my own experience in my own family and the people in my book are real" ("Trumpet I"). Thus Lowry's own siblings, parents, and grandparents become those of the narrator, Elizabeth Lorimer. "David," who is hospitalized in San Diego, is Lowry's own cousin who returned shell-shocked from World War II. Judge Crandall is her grandfather's friend Judge Biddle, who had already appeared in "The Recital."

Her grandfather's cook, Fleta Jordan, became the basis for "Tatie," one of Lowry's favorite characters. "She was a remarkable woman," Lowry explains, "and when that book was finished . . . I took it back to that little town in Pennsylvania." Lowry sought out Jordan's house down by the railroad station, where her grandfather had taken young Lois and Helen to see the seven o'clock train come through, and gave her a copy. At the time, Jordan was ninety-five years old and "could not understand why someone would have written a book about her."[23]

Like Lowry, Elizabeth Jane Lorimer, the novel's narrator, moves to Pennsylvania to live with her grandparents at the age of six when World War II steals her father away. Elizabeth also resembles her creator in other ways: She is an accomplished artist, learns to read when she is four years old, and has a March birthday. Lowry identifies enough with Elizabeth that, in a cover illustration for a paperback edition of *Autumn Street*, she asked the artist to give Elizabeth blonde instead of dark hair, even though this detail is never specified in the text (Chaston 1994).

Many of the specific plot elements in *Autumn Street* stem directly from Lowry's experience. One scene, for example, occurred much as described in the novel: Elizabeth helps Tatie sign her autograph book because she finally realizes that the maid cannot write. Tatie's grandson, Charles, who is murdered, was modeled after Fleta Jordan's granddaughter, Gloria, who was killed when she was 17 under somewhat different circumstances. Like Elizabeth's stepgrandmother, Lowry's also caused a stir by attending the funeral of her maid's grandchild at an all-black church.

When Lowry first submitted *Autumn Street* to her publisher, "they held it for a long time because they didn't quite know what to do with it. There was some feeling that it ought to be published as an adult book" (Ross, 335). Although it was finally released as a children's title, Lowry often receives letters from adults who have inadvertently picked it up and discovered their own childhoods. Indeed, the novel was originally reviewed in the *New Yorker* with no mention that it was published for children. Widely praised by reviewers, *Autumn Street* was an American Library Association Notable Book and was named to the IBBY (International Board on Books for Young People) Honor List.

Because readers had been clamoring for another "Anastasia" book, Lowry published in 1981 a second novel about the Krupniks, *Anastasia Again!* Now 12 years old, Anastasia is aghast that her family has decided to leave their Cambridge apartment and move to a suburb of Boston. In 1983, *Anastasia Again!* was a nominee in the juvenile paperback category of the American Book Award.

Lowry has continued the phenomenally popular series, allowing Anastasia to experience the seventh and eighth grades and face problems such as taking care of her family while her mother is away, trying to climb the rope in gym class, agonizing over a future career, and searching for romance through a newspaper advertisement. The series includes *Anastasia at Your Service* (1982), *Anastasia, Ask Your Analyst*

(1984), *Anastasia on Her Own* (1985), *Anastasia Has the Answers* (1986), *Anastasia's Chosen Career* (1987), *Anastasia at This Address* (1991), and *Anastasia, Absolutely* (1995). Especially with the publication of *Anastasia Krupnik* and its early sequels, Lowry began to gain a following of loyal readers. For a time she invented a fictional secretary, Marion Kline, who could do uncomfortable tasks for her, such as turning down requests to read manuscripts by aspiring writers (Smith, 153).

In 1983 Lowry and Small bought an old farmhouse in Sanbornton, New Hampshire. Lowry explains that one day she and Martin Small were driving down a road and came across a house that matched the one she had described in *A Summer to Die*. It was even built the same year, 1840. As a result she bought it and now uses it on weekends and in the summer, allowing her to live a double life, enjoying the pleasures of both city and country life ("Visit").

That same year, *The One Hundredth Thing About Caroline*, the first of three books about the Tate family, appeared. Lowry created the Tates partly in response to letters from parents and teachers asking for a book about children who, unlike Anastasia, have divorced parents. The novel focuses on Caroline Tate, aptly described as an "Anastasia-like character" with "a strong sense of who she is and who she wants to be—a verte-brate paleontologist specializing in Mesozoic dinosaurs."[24] One of the characters in this book, a reporter for *People* magazine named Michael Small, is a real-life individual, Martin Small's nephew, who at the time actually worked for the magazine.[25] Caroline Tate would appear again in *Switcharound* (1985), in which she and her brother, J. P., visit their father in Des Moines, Iowa. Another book about the Tates, *Your Move, J. P.* (1989), was written in response to requests for a book with a male pro-tagonist and focuses on J. P.

Lowry has created several other humorous books that have been well received. *Taking Care of Terrific* (1983) is set in and around Beacon Hill, where Lowry lived for many years. The novel began to develop one evening when Lowry and a friend were in the Boston Public Garden as the famous "swan boats" were being chained up for the evening. Lowry wondered who would possibly try to steal the boats, and on the way home she started devising the plot for the novel.[26] In 1987, *Taking Care of Terrific* was made into a film for the *Wonderworks* television series.

Us and Uncle Fraud (1984) was partly inspired by one of Lowry's great-uncles, an eccentric man who had married her grandfather's sister. "In those long ago safe days of childhood," Lowry reminisces, "I would go downtown by myself and buy a new set of paperdolls at the five and ten and then I would stop into Uncle Frank's law office. He'd always be there alone . . . and would tell me funny stories and sing me funny songs. I remember him singing, 'The monkey he got drunk and sat on the elephant's trunk.' He was full of poems and great charm for a child, sort of a magical uncle" (Chaston 1994). Long after Lowry was grown and her uncle was dead, her parents told her that "Uncle Frank was such a flighty, whimsical fey character that he couldn't [have] a law practice." Afraid that he might actually take a real case, "the family got together and they paid for his office and paid him a salary in return for him never practicing law. He just sat there and wrote poetry and things. He was just kind of somebody off another planet, but he was magical to me" (Chaston 1994).

One of Lowry's most widely praised novels—and one of her personal favorites—*Rabble Starkey*, was published in 1987. For some years, Lowry had visited her brother, Jon, who is now a doctor, and his family, who live in rural Virginia, the setting of *Rabble Starkey*. Lowry explains, "During that period, I was hearing a lot about the large number of pregnant teenagers; children having children. . . . So I began to think about writing the book from the point of view of a kid who has been born to a kid" (Miller, 138). The resulting book, *Rabble Starkey*, won the *Boston Globe-Horn Book* Award for fiction and the Golden Kite Award for fiction from the Society of Children's Book Writers.

Ever since the first Anastasia book appeared, Lowry had received a number of requests from children who wanted a book about Anastasia's younger brother, Sam. Lowry had talked about the idea with her editor but initially agreed it was silly because "Sam was very little and three-year-olds aren't going to read a novel about Sam, but thirteen-year-olds don't want to read a book about a three-year-old, or so we thought" (Chaston 1994). The idea intrigued Lowry enough, however, that she wrote *All about Sam*, published in 1988, a sort of history of Sam's early years. Around this time, Lois's first grandchild was born and helped inspire Sam's adventures.[27] The book has proved very popular with fans of Anastasia and with younger readers as well. A second book about Sam, *Attaboy, Sam!*, appeared in 1992, followed by *See You Around, Sam!* in 1996.

Two Newbery Awards

In the spring of 1988, Lowry took a vacation with an old friend, Annelise Platt. The two women had met years before when their former husbands were law partners, but their time together had been "interrupted by jobs or friends or children."[28] During the week they spent in a small guest house in Bermuda, the two women talked about their childhoods. Platt had grown up in Copenhagen, Denmark, during World War II, eventually marrying an American army officer. Although they had talked of the hostilities before, Lowry writes, "This time, for the first time, talking of the past, I became truly aware of the way her childhood was colored by war" ("Newbery 1990," 416). Lowry was deeply affected by the stories Annelise told. "Of course, my childhood was affected by the war," Lowry explains, "but in such a superficial way. I've known other people who've lived in war-torn places as it were, but I've never really heard anybody talk about what it felt like to be little, scared . . . to live in a place where you were under that hostile military situation" (Chaston 1994). What interested Lowry were the details of Platt's story: the Nazis with their heavy boots walking the streets of Copenhagen, the mittens her friend wore to bed because of the cold. Platt also related the story of how the Danes had smuggled the Jewish population out of Denmark in October of 1943.

Convinced that the rescue of the Jews from Denmark could be told for children "in a fictional way that would put the reader right there with a frightened, brave, proud little Danish girl," Lowry began—with Platt's permission—to write a story drawing from her friend's experiences.[29] As she worked on the manuscript, Lowry realized that she needed to develop a more tangible feel for Copenhagen. In Denmark, Lowry visited the place where Resistance fighters had been executed and took the train north of Copenhagen to look across the ocean to Sweden as her characters do in the novel. She also talked to people who had experienced the war, including some who had been involved in the Danish Resistance.

Number the Stars was published in 1989 and sparked a great deal of critical attention. The novel received the Sydney Taylor Award from the Association of Jewish Libraries and the National Jewish Book Award the following year. It has also won a number of state children's book awards, including the Charlie May Simon Award (Arkansas), the Charlotte Award (New York), the Dorothy Canfield Fisher Children's Book Award (Vermont), the Golden Archer Award (Wisconsin), the Indian Paintbrush Award (Wyoming), and the Rebecca Caudill Young Reader's Book Award (Illinois). In January of 1990, the novel received the prestigious John Newbery Medal, sponsored by the American Library Association. Lowry was then immediately asked to appear on the *Today Show,* although it meant traveling through a bad snowstorm to New York. She arrived after getting only a few hours of sleep and was bumped from the program in the eastern time zone for a space shuttle launch. *Number the Stars* has become a best-selling book, both in hardback and paperback, and has been widely embraced by school teachers in the United States and abroad.

In 1993, Lowry's mother passed away after a period of illness during which she eventually went blind. During the last year or two of her life, she would relate tales about her childhood during Lowry's visits. Lowry's father was in the same nursing home in a separate section and, while in better physical condition, was losing his memory. Lowry explains, "There was that phenomenon of seeing someone who had involuntarily released all of his memories and lost them and down the hall here was the person who was blind and on oxygen and still continued all those stories and memories" (Chaston 1994). This ironic situation became in part the impetus for Lowry's *The Giver* (1993), her dystopian novel about the power and importance of memory.

Almost immediately after publication, *The Giver* attracted praise from critics, including an almost unprecedented editorial in *The Horn Book* by Anita Silvey and an article in a subsequent issue by Patty Campbell. Silvey and Campbell both felt that in writing *The Giver* Lowry took a successful risk by experimenting with a type of book unlike any of the others she had written. As a result, in 1994 Lowry joined Joseph Krumgold, Elizabeth George Speare, and Katherine Paterson as one of the few to win the Newbery Award twice.[30] This time, when the award was announced, Lowry and Martin Small were on a boat in the Weddell Sea as part of a trip to Antarctica, which was a present for Small's retirement. In addition to the Newbery Medal, *The Giver* has received a variety of other honors, including the Regina Medal and the following citations: a *Boston Globe-Horn Book* Honor Book, American Library Association Notable Children's Book, American Library Association Best Book for Young Adults, National Council of Teachers of English Notable Book in the Language Arts, *Horn Book* Fanfare, and International Reading Association-Children's Book Council Choice.

An Ordinary Life

According to Lowry, her current life is fairly ordinary. In 1993 she and Martin Small moved to a house in Cambridge, about six blocks from the apartment where she and her family had once lived. Like Anastasia, who walks her new dog in *Anastasia, Absolutely*, Lowry spends her early mornings exercising Bandit, a Tibetan terrier. Most days she writes for around five hours, often working on more than one project at a time. She spends a great deal of time thinking about a book before writing it and then works on it a chapter at a time, rewriting each before going on to the next one.

Lowry still spends weekends at her home in New Hampshire. She enjoys what she has described as the hobbies of stereotypical grand-mothers: knitting, growing flowers, and baking cookies.[31] Although still an avid reader, she does not spend much time reading children's books. She enjoys adult books featuring mature women with whom she can relate and literary biographies and memoirs. Most of Lowry's personal life is quite separate from her career as a children's author, although she corresponds regularly with children's writers, such as Phyllis Reynolds Naylor and Marion Dane Bauer.

To those familiar with the dramatic quality of her novels, it will come as no surprise that Lowry is an inveterate, albeit sometimes indiscrimi-nate, moviegoer. She describes herself as the only person over 50 who willingly went to see *Wayne's World II*. When I visited her in 1994, she had already gone to three movies that week and planned on seeing another that evening. Lowry is especially fond of films by screenwriter Horton Foote, including *To Kill a Mockingbird* (1962), *Tomorrow* (1983), and *The Trip to Bountiful* (1985).

Lowry and Martin Small also enjoy traveling for pleasure, not just in order to promote her books. She muses that as she gets older, she and Small have found themselves doing "strangely adventurous things" like rafting down the Colorado River for eight days or journeying to the bot-tom of the world (Chaston 1994). Among other places, they have trav-eled to Africa, Norway, Hawaii, and Antarctica.

Lowry is still very much involved in the lives of her children and grandchildren, whom she discusses with great pride. Her oldest daugh-ter, Alix, graduated from Vassar and then worked on a doctorate in eco-nomics. She left graduate school to pursue what Lowry describes as "a meteoric career" in computers until, at the age of 28, she was diagnosed with a fairly debilitating form of multiple sclerosis. Alix lived in Boston for a number of years until relocating to San Francisco. For some years, Lowry's son Grey was a pilot in the Air Force serving in Germany. He eventually married a native German, Margret, who gave birth to a daughter, Nadine, in 1993. Tragically, in May of 1995, Grey was killed in an airplane crash while on duty. "I've been through a very tough year," Lowry said of her son's death. "I made a book using photographs for my granddaughter, who is so young she won't remember her father."[32] Lowry's daughter Kristin, mother of Lowry's first grandchild, James Norton, lives in Kittery, Maine. Lowry's son Benjamin, who "wanted to be a professional baseball player, but peaked in the minors," is now a successful lawyer in Portland, Maine, where he works with his father.

In a brief essay in the *Horn Book*, written when Lowry won her second Newbery Prize, Walter Lorraine noted Lowry's unique ability to write both humorous and serious fiction. Although praising *The Giver*, he writes, "I am absolutely convinced that Lois's best book is yet to come. I am looking forward to it."[33] Given Lowry's career, it seems likely that such a book will be different from anything else she has written. She has, she explains, always been encouraged to experiment, to keep from turning out the same book over and over again (Chaston 1994). Ultimately, Lowry has already established an important body of work, one that will undoubtedly earn her a niche as one of the most popular and significant twentieth-century American writers for children, a spot that is a direct result of her "inward eye."

Chapter Two
Early Novels:
Return to Autumn Street

Lowry, who had been creating stories and poems since childhood, seemed destined to become a writer. After all, her high school yearbook had pegged her as a "future novelist" and she had studied creative writing in college. While raising her family, Lowry's desire to write did not wane; instead, she created occasional stories for her children. When Lowry went back to school, finally completing her degree and beginning graduate studies, she began a career as a freelance nonfiction writer and photographer that lasted through her eventual divorce and relocation to Boston in 1978.

Although children figure prominently in several of her articles and stories of that period, none of Lowry's earliest published writing was intended for young readers. Even her first novels, especially *A Summer to Die* and *Autumn Street*, have what might be described as an adult tone or, as in the case of *Anastasia Krupnik*, employ adult humor, as she evidently grappled for a time with the question of audience.

A Summer to Die (1977)

When Melanie Kroupa of Houghton Mifflin wrote to Lowry, encouraging her to write a manuscript for children, Lowry turned to the same source material—her own life—that she had used as a basis for two short stories in the mid-1970s, "Crow Call" and "The Recital." It had been 15 years since Lowry's sister, Helen, had passed away, but Lowry could still vividly remember the experience as well as the sibling rivalry she had felt as a child. In completing her first novel, *A Summer to Die*, Lowry drew on real feelings and events. Like Molly in the book, Helen was beautiful and popular, characteristics that at times might have been difficult for a younger, more insecure, sister.

A Summer to Die is one of only four of Lowry's novels written from the first-person point of view. The narrator, 13-year-old Meg Chalmers, is Lowry herself at a younger age. An artist and a budding photographer,

Meg is a gifted child who does not recognize her own self-worth. In many ways, Meg's older sister Molly, who is 15, is her polar opposite. To Meg, it seems as if, in attempting to get a "whole, well-put-together person," her parents had to come up with two daughters. Molly is "calm, easygoing, self-confident, downright smug."[1] She is also a pretty cheerleader who claims many boyfriends and who assumes that good things will just happen to her. She can lose graciously when the sisters play Monopoly because she always wins in the things she cares about. On the other hand, Meg sees herself as "hasty, impetuous, sometimes angry over nothing, often miserable about everything" (*Summer,* 3). It is because Molly is neat and Meg throws crumpled-up papers with unfinished poems onto the floor that the older sister has drawn a line with blue chalk down the middle of the room.

Up until the point that the novel begins, Meg has not been forced to live in such close quarters with Molly. The Chalmers family has only recently moved to an old house in an unidentified part of the New England countryside (not too distant from a hospital in Portland, Maine). Dr. Chalmers, like the father of Lowry's most well-known creation, Anastasia Krupnik, is an English professor. In order to finish writing a book, *The Dialectic Synthesis of Irony*, he has moved the family to the countryside. Neither of his daughters has been excited about the move: Molly has to give up cheerleading, and Meg can no longer take Saturday morning photography classes.

While the Chalmerses are living in the country, Molly becomes ill with what turns out to be acute myelogenous leukemia and eventually dies. Much of the book deals with the impact on Meg of Molly's illness and death, which coincides with Meg's own growth both as an individual and as an artist. Meg comes to appreciate her sister and gains confidence in herself through three new adult friends. The first, Will Banks, is an older man who owns the house the Chalmerses are renting and who encourages Meg's interest in photography, recognizing her talents, lending her an old German camera with several lenses. At the end of the book, a photograph of Meg that Will has taken appears in a display at the university where Meg's father teaches. As Meg explains, Will's picture "had captured . . . and made permanent whatever of Molly was in me," helping her to see that her sister is still alive in her (*Summer,* 151). Meg, who has always felt insecure about her looks, partly because of her sister, recognizes that Will has made her feel beautiful. Will counters this idea, however, in the novel's last line: "Meg, . . . you were beautiful all along" (*Summer,* 154).

Although several of Lowry's books include the death of a major character, they usually feature an accompanying birth, suggesting the cyclical nature of life. In *A Summer to Die*, an infant boy is born to two college students, Ben Brady and Maria Abbott, neighbors of the Chalmerses and friends to Meg. While Molly is slowly dying in the hospital, Ben and Maria's baby is delivered, much like Lowry's own son, Ben, who came into the world while her sister Helen was dying. Meg shares in the joy of this birth, which takes place at home, and, at Ben and Maria's request, she photographs the event.

Through Molly's death, Meg begins to grow up, learning that she cannot pretend that bad things will not happen. This idea is expressed through Ben's statement to Meg that "you can *pretend* that bad things will never happen. But life's a lot easier if you realize and admit that sometimes they do" (*Summer,* 105–6). Ben's remarks anger Meg; she does not think that one ought to anticipate bad things. However, at the very end of the novel, Meg writes that she now understands what Ben has said and that she knows instinctively that one day Will Banks will be gone as well.

As in almost every Lowry book that will follow, *A Summer to Die* also treats both the joy and pain that come from memory. Initially, Lowry suggests this concept through the patchwork quilt that Meg's mother is making from pieces of the family's old clothes. The use of a quilt to symbolize a family's memories is a motif that forms the basis for several other children's books, most notably Valerie Flournoy's *The Patchwork Quilt* (1985), winner of the Coretta Scott King Award. For both Meg and Molly, the quilt is an embarrassment, reminding them of some unpleasant memories. As Meg explains, "let's face it, some memories are better off forgotten, especially when you haven't lived far enough from them yet" (*Summer,* 38). Because they have not "lived far enough" from their memories after Molly dies, Meg's parents will not think of returning to the same house the following summer. Yet, as time passes, Meg is able to recall memories of her sister that, much like the photographs she has been taking, help keep her alive. This realization dawns on Meg at the very end of the novel when Will Banks accompanies her to the woods near his house. Standing in a field of flowers, Meg can recall Molly. "In my mind," Meg explains, "in quick sequences as if a film were stopping and starting, I saw Molly again. I saw her standing in the grass when it was green, her arms full of flowers; with the wind in her hair, with her quick smile, reaching for the next flower, and the next. . . . Somewhere, for Molly, I thought suddenly, it would be summer still, summer always" (*Summer,* 153–54).

Lowry's first attempt at writing for children certainly validated the faith of her publishers, although her manuscript did undergo some routine revisions before being published. On September 14, 1976, Melanie Kroupa of Houghton Mifflin wrote to tell Lowry that she found the manuscript promising and sensitive. She also suggested revisions for the novel dealing with character development and a few key scenes, including the birth Meg witnesses and the very ending.[2] The manuscript for this book had also originally included a longer title, *A Season to Flower, A Summer to Die*.[3]

The resulting book was a critical success. Both the *Horn Book* and the *Junior Bookshelf* called the book "sensitive" and praised Lowry's style.[4] *School Library Journal* went on to suggest that "the story captures the mysteries of living and dying, without manipulating the reader's emotions, providing understanding and a comforting sense of completion."[5] More recently, Jeanne Bracken and Sharon Wigutoff have criticized the book for its use of caricatures and "stereotyping of female and male sex roles."[6]

On one level, *A Summer to Die* is a spare, fairly simple book and an easy read. What stands out about the book are the thoughts and emotions of the main character who is at once likable and credible. *A Summer to Die* earned Lowry the International Reading Association's Children's Book Award, given annually for a first or second book for children, the first of many awards for her work. In addition, the book received two state awards for children's and young adult literature: the California Young Reader Medal, High School, and the Massachusetts Children's Book Award, both in 1981.

Find a Stranger, Say Goodbye (1978)

Lowry's second novel, *Find a Stranger, Say Goodbye*, like *A Summer to Die*, involves an attempt at understanding the past as well as coming to terms with personal problems through memory. Beautiful, popular Natalie Armstrong, the novel's protagonist, is at first much more like Molly than Meg Chalmers. All of her many friends expect her to become a success as she graduates from high school. Natalie also has successful parents. Her father, Alden, is understanding and supportive; her mother, Kay, is vibrant and spontaneous, and Natalie loves her. Even her younger sister, Nancy, is likable. There is virtually no sibling rivalry between the sisters—certainly none of Meg Chalmers's jealousy. The Armstrongs live comfortably in the town of Branford, Maine. Alden

Armstrong is a respected physician, and Natalie plans on following in his footsteps. In fact, in most respects Natalie's life is almost too good to be true.

Natalie's one problem is that, since she is adopted, she has no known past. "Sometimes I lie awake at night, wondering what the story is behind my birth," she explains in the first draft of an essay she must write to get into MacKenzie College.[7] Natalie longs to know the history of her birth parents, hoping that, as a result, she will better understand her own physical and mental characteristics. To discover who she really is, Natalie embarks on a search for her past, one that parallels Joseph Campbell's "monomyth," the hero-quest story found in virtually every culture.[8]

As a graduation present, Natalie's adoptive parents give her the means to embark on her quest: special "weapons" (a bank account and her adoption documents) and a trusty "steed" (a car her father has leased). Natalie first stops at the island home of her adoptive grandmother, Tallie, an eccentric artist who becomes her mentor and provides important counsel. Tallie encourages Natalie to find out everything she can about her birth parents. "But there simply isn't any choice when you know you have to do something," she tells Natalie (*Stranger*, 52). She assures Natalie, ". . . you'll find your own past. If you like what you find, embrace it. If you don't, shrug it away" (*Stranger*, 53). Her grandmother gives her a gift that provides some insight into her own past, letters that Kay Armstrong wrote to Tallie about adopting Natalie. Although Natalie does not recognize it at the time, her grandmother has provided her with her "true" identity, that of a beloved, adopted daughter of a caring family.

The letters Kay Armstrong has written are filled with fairy-tale imagery. For example, the infant Natalie, Kay writes, resembles the Sleeping Beauty in a fairy-tale book she once received from Tallie. She also mentions a painting by Tallie's second husband, Stefan, of a nude Red Riding Hood, which Natalie also remembers. The picture, she recalls, was filled with hidden things, including the wolf who was part of the forest. When she was younger, Natalie had longed to warn the innocent child in the painting about the wolf. Now, Natalie, who is herself journeying from innocence into experience, is not aware of the dangers she may face in her own search.

Natalie then travels to Simmons' Mills, a small town in the "north-central mountainous section of the state," to talk to Foster H. Goodwin, the attorney who arranged for her adoption (*Stranger,* 45). To Natalie, this part of her investigation seems like "a trip into a primeval time" (*Stranger,* 71). Unfortunately for Natalie, Foster H. Goodwin is dead. Clarence Therrian, the doctor who delivered her, is still alive, however, although he lies ill in a hospital. When she visits him, he mistakes her for her own birth mother, Julie Jeffries, who, he reveals, was 15 years old when she gave birth. With this bit of knowledge, Natalie tries to find out everything she can about Julie, checking an old high school year-book and newspapers from 1959 and 1960. After a series of phone calls (to the P. R. Simmons Paper Company in Simmons' Mills and the Wentworth Manufacturing Company in Philadelphia, where Julie's father had worked, to Miss Sheridan's school in Connecticut, where Julie had transferred, and to an Episcopal church in Glen Sevren, Pennsylvania), Natalie finally obtains the phone number of Julie's own mother but cannot bring herself to call her.

Meanwhile, Tallie has become ill, and her daughter has to care for her. Like Lowry's Anastasia Krupnik, who must run the house while her own mother is gone in *Anastasia on Her Own,* Natalie has to take on her mother's domestic responsibilities, becoming "a list-making grouch" (*Stranger,* 119). During this time, Natalie finally calls Margaret Jeffries, Julie's mother, by posing as one of Julie's old classmates, and she learns that her birth mother is a model, married, the mother of two children, and living on East 79th Street in New York City.

In the last stage of Natalie's search, she travels to New York to meet Julie. Natalie has never been to the big city before and, innocently, has chosen to stay in "one of Manhattan's finest old hotels" near Central Park, which turns out to be quite expensive (*Stranger,* 125). Natalie is relieved that Julie is willing to meet her and the two arrange to have lunch in the Russian Tea Room. When Julie arrives at the restaurant she is able to recognize Natalie because they look so much alike. "Looking at you," Julie tells Natalie, "is like having a mirror into the past" (*Stranger,* 135). Natalie soon begins to realize that Julie is quite superficial, especially when she suddenly decides that Natalie should give up her aspirations of becoming a doctor to work as a model.

The most important result of the lunch is that Julie offers to let Natalie read the diary she kept when she became pregnant. The diary entries reveal a lonely teenager, a newcomer to a small town, who becomes attracted to a college student named Terry. In a subsequent visit to Julie's apartment, Natalie learns that her birth father, Terry, was killed in an accident shortly after her birth, and that Doctor Therrian was Terry's father. Despite the insight that the diary provides, Natalie realizes that, aside from a physical resemblance, she has little in common with Julie.

Natalie returns to Branford to find that Tallie, who is recuperating, is staying at her house. Tallie, Kay, Natalie, and Nancy soon become involved in a discussion about the importance of memory. If Tallie could choose anyplace to be, it would be in the past because "there are all these memories that I yearn sometimes to go back to" (*Stranger,* 163). When Nancy responds that memories are sometimes better than the past really was, Kay interjects that this is because "you can filter out the bad parts" (*Stranger,* 163). Tallie then suggests that the important thing with memory is to use it selectively.

As a result of her search, Natalie returns to her family with a clearer sense of herself. Unlike one of her father's patients, Natalie has learned to say goodbye to her past. Telling her father about finding Julie, Natalie explains, "I said hello to her, and I said goodbye to her. I won't *forget* her. But she's not part of my life anymore" (*Stranger,* 171). Natalie does, however, return to Simmons' Mills to see Dr. Therrian, who is dying, because he had cried when the lawyer took the infant Natalie away.

At the end of the novel, Natalie, much like Tallie with her selective memory, concludes that growing up boils down to knowing what to hang onto and what to toss away. "You have to acknowledge what is and what was," she tells herself. "And sometimes what never was, at all" (*Stranger,* 187). At this point, Natalie recalls the Green Panther lamp, a repulsive gift the Armstrongs once received from Aunt Helen. The family had placed it on top of the television and tried to ignore it. Ultimately, Natalie's mother had broken it, calmly explaining that if something is invisible, "you are very apt to bump into it very hard with your elbow" (*Stranger,* 9). For Natalie, the question of her parentage has always been there, much like the lamp, invisible, overlooked by her whole family. Now, like the lamp, she can throw away that which is broken. Symbolically, Natalie crumples up a picture of Julie that appeared on the cover of *Vogue* and tosses it out, along with other useless treasures from her high school years. This "housecleaning" continues until the room is "bare of everything except the memories; those would always be there, Natalie knew" (*Stranger,* 187).[9]

At first glance, *Find a Stranger, Say Goodbye* seems a somewhat typical novel about adoption. Indeed, a number of other novels about young adults torn between their birth and adoptive mothers have appeared in the last few years. In Caroline B. Cooney's *The Face on the Milk Carton*

(1990) and its sequel, *Whatever Happened to Janie?* (1993), another teenage girl must decide who her "real" parents are, a decision made all the more difficult since she was kidnapped from her birth parents. Despite many other novels about the subject, however, *Find a Stranger, Say Goodbye* continues to speak to young readers partly because it deals with a young adult who, despite a kind, loving adoptive family, feels the urge to learn about her birth parents anyway. At the same time, although most of the novel is presented from Natalie's point of view, both her adoptive mother—through her letters—and her birth mother—through her diary—have a voice in the story. Whereas the adult Julie is a fairly flat character, the younger Julie speaks for many young adults who are forced to make complicated decisions and who face crises as teenagers.

Lowry has received a variety of interesting responses to this novel from her readers. A class of unmarried, pregnant teenagers in Detroit was asked to read *Find a Stranger, Say Goodbye,* and their teacher sent Lowry a collection of letters they had written. Almost without exception, the students were upset with the novel's ending because "it implied that the natural mother had made the right choice in giving up the baby to mature and competent parents." One of these letters, Lowry says, nearly broke her heart. The girl wrote, "I'm going to be a better mother to this baby than my mother ever was to me," which, given her present circumstances, seemed unlikely (Chaston 1994).

Other readers have also written to Lowry, wishing that she had changed the novel's ending. Lowry has, on many occasions, written back to them that "a book can end any number of ways and the author can only choose one. I could have chosen ending 'a,' 'c,' 'd,' or 'y,' but I chose 'b.' And I'm sorry if they want 'f,' but I couldn't do it all ways." Lowry has sometimes referred readers to P. D. James's novel *Innocent Blood* (1988), which deals with a similar subject. In that book "a young girl of eighteen . . . tracks down her natural parents and discovers they were serving a life sentence in prison for the sex murder of a small child—so that's just ending 'x.'. . . [T]here's an infinite realm of endings in a book like that and you're bound to disappoint people. A lot of people wanted the girl and the natural mother to ride off into the sunset together. I tried hard to reflect what really might be" (Chaston 1994).

The initial response to *Find a Stranger, Say Goodbye* was mixed. Both Marjorie Lewis and David Rees criticized the book for its romanticized, sentimental view of life, whereas Ethel L. Heins argued that *Find a Stranger, Say Goodbye* "is the kind of novel that reminds the reader that realism can often be less of an honest revelation of life than fantasy."[10] On the other hand, Lance Salway maintains that the novel's "overly romantic elements are essential to [Lowry's] purpose. Her 'message' is that filial love has nothing to do with biology, that one loves one's parents because they love you and want you and care for you, not because they created you."[11] *Find a Stranger, Say Goodbye* has proved a popular book with young readers and was cited in a 1979 Books for Young Adults poll published in the *English Journal*.[12] In 1980, *Find a Stranger, Say Goodbye* was adapted as an *NBC Special Treats* television special. This adaptation, however, left out many key elements, changed the setting to California, and is one that Lowry says she would rather forget.

Autumn Street (1980)

After completing *Find a Stranger, Say Goodbye,* Lowry began writing her most autobiographical book, *Autumn Street,* which was not actually published until after the first of her "Anastasia" books, *Anastasia Krupnik. Autumn Street* draws heavily on Lowry's experiences in Carlisle, Pennsylvania, during World War II. As in *A Summer to Die,* Lowry explores the subjects of death and grief.

Initially, Lowry's publisher was reluctant to publish *Autumn Street* because of questions about its intended audience. Lowry recalls taking back the manuscript in an attempt to make it more marketable. "I wrote whole new chunks of that book," Lowry says, interspersing the previous material with scenes featuring an 18-year-old Elizabeth, an art student in Boston who is thinking about dropping out of school (Chaston 1994). As a result of this decision, the adult Elizabeth is seeing a psychiatrist, who elicits the story of her childhood from her. Lowry maintains that, with the "interjection of the eighteen-year-old, it could then become a book for young adults" (Chaston 1994). The publisher held on to the book, agonizing over it, and eventually rejected the new version, publishing the manuscript as originally written.

Lowry admits that the book is an "aberration" that "doesn't fit into any category," yet argues that it *has* stayed in print and that some adults love it.[13] Occasionally, Lowry receives letters from adults who have come across it and who feel that the book has captured some of their own feelings about growing up. One fourth-grade teacher in Illinois reads the book to his class every year and writes what Lowry describes as an "annual love letter." "He loves that book," Lowry says, "and the way that children respond to it" (Chaston 1994). As evidence, she points to a letter from one of his students who says that if she could choose any-place to be from any book, it would be *Autumn Street*. For Lowry, this response suggests "that with a good teacher, it's a book that can work with kids, but no nine-year-old is going to pick it up and say, 'Here's a Lois Lowry book! Wow! I love this' " (Chaston 1994).

Except for the novel's prologue, the action focuses on the year that Elizabeth, the narrator, is six, and it ends with her seventh birthday. After the Japanese attack on Pearl Harbor, Elizabeth's father goes off to war, and her mother leaves New York, taking her and her older, more graceful, sister, Jessica, to live in her grandfather's house in Pennsylvania. Already apprehensive about the move, Elizabeth does not care for her stepgrandmother and is afraid that she will not make friends in her new town. Much of the book focuses on her relationship with the cook, Tatie, who becomes a sort of surrogate grandmother, and Tatie's grandson, Charles, who, at the end of the book, is murdered by an apparently mentally ill vagrant named Ferdie Gossett. At the time of the murder, Elizabeth contracts pneumonia, from which she eventually recovers just as her father returns home. He promises her that nothing bad will ever happen again, a statement that she and her father both recognize as a lie, but one that they desperately need.

Much like *A Summer to Die*, the novel is an initiation story, one in which the innocent Elizabeth is introduced to death in a number of separate incidents. Autumn Street, where the action takes place, is appropriately named. Despite the joy that Elizabeth finds in her friendships with Tatie and Charles, the innocence of spring and summer is fast changing to autumn, full of constant reminders of the fragile nature of life.

As is the case with Lowry's earlier novels, *Autumn Street* is concerned with the importance of memory and perception, a theme announced in an epigram by e. e. cummings, which appears on the dedication page: "[A]long the brittle treacherous bright streets of memory comes my heart."[14] The book begins with a prologue, reminiscent of sections in Harper Lee's *To Kill a Mockingbird* (1960), another of Lowry's favorite childhood books, and the opening of Katherine Paterson's Newbery Award-winning *Jacob Have I Loved* (1980), which was published the same year as *Autumn Street*. Like these other works, *Autumn Street* employs an adult narrator who is reexamining her early childhood memories. "It was a long time ago," Elizabeth explains, sorting through her recollections (*Autumn*, 1). Still artistic, the adult Elizabeth contemplates painting Autumn Street, where her grandfather once lived, but recognizes that her view will "be distorted and askew" as it was when she was six. Elizabeth goes on to describe how she would paint the people she associates with Autumn Street: her grandmother and grandfather, Noah, Charles, and the cook, Tatie. Because most of them are probably now dead, Elizabeth paints them in the sky above as if they were angels; indeed, Noah and Charles, both children, die in the course of the novel. Later, when a visiting professor of education falls in love with Elizabeth's paintings, the professor and Elizabeth's own teacher talk about "Elizabeth's perceptions" (*Autumn*, 13). Her changing images of the world around her occupy most of the rest of the book.

Like many children, Elizabeth initially accepts much of what others tell her, often developing erroneous notions about life. She believes, for example, that if her expectant mother gives birth to a baby boy, her father will die, since a family friend, Judge Crandall, has pronounced that during times of war male children are born to replace the soldiers who are killed. Elizabeth also believes that the Japanese beetles infesting the trees around her grandfather's house have been sent by the Japanese who are at war with the United States. She readily accepts Charles's assertion that children do not die and another child's statement that the woods at the end of Autumn Street are filled with escaped pet turtles, now grown to gigantic size. Quick to judge others, Elizabeth initially thinks that Charles will not make a good playmate and that Tatie is, after all, "only the cook" (*Autumn*, 17). Elizabeth also has what Tatie describes as a prejudice against her grandmother, whom she assumes has no compassion.

Eventually, most of Elizabeth's "preconceived notions," like those of Lowry's Anastasia in *Anastasia Again*, prove false. Charles becomes Elizabeth's best friend, and she announces that she wants to marry him. When Tatie becomes her confidante and mentor, Elizabeth seeks to protect her. In a moment drawn from Lowry's own life, Elizabeth, who has come to idealize Tatie, learns from her grandmother that Tatie cannot read or write. In an attempt to prove her grandmother wrong and change the real world, Elizabeth guides Tatie's hands so that she can sign her autograph book. Elizabeth's grandmother also redeems herself by overcoming her own prejudices and attending Charles's funeral at the all-black Full Gospel Church. Recounting the event, Tatie explains that Elizabeth's grandmother's eyes teared, and "and she no more care, right then, what color she is, or I am" (*Autumn*, 186).

In *Autumn Street,* many of the characters' preconceptions center around gender, race, and social class. Early in the book, Elizabeth wants to become a boy, thinking that she can rather easily change her gender and that, in doing so, she can somehow protect her father. Later, she and Charles try to determine whether the next-door neighbors, the Hoffmans, who are Germans, might be spies. Much of the book, as in Katherine Paterson's other Newbery Award-winning novel, *Bridge to Terabithia* (1977), details the friendship of a boy and girl from different social backgrounds, one of whom eventually dies. At first, Elizabeth does not realize the social implications of the fact that she comes from a wealthy, privileged, Episcopalian, white family and that Charles is the son of a working-class, single black mother. The children are quite innocent, oblivious of their differences, even willing to show each other their underpants. Elizabeth cannot understand why Charles is not allowed to attend her school or why she has never seen Tatie's house. When Elizabeth's great-aunts take an interest in Charles on his birthday, however, she becomes jealous and, mimicking adults she has evidently overheard, she tells him, "Happy birthday, nigger" (*Autumn,* 98). In the culmination of several scenes in which Charles and Elizabeth seem to be growing apart, the racial taunts of other children result in Charles's determination to go to the woods at the end of Autumn Street, where he is killed. When Elizabeth goes off to Jefferson School to begin first grade, she makes another friend, Louise Donohue, whose mother evidently resents the fact that Elizabeth's family has money.

Toward the end of the story, Elizabeth begins to realize that the racial and social boundaries that separate people are misleading, even destructive. Rejecting the prejudices of the adults around her, Elizabeth explains, "I decided that we were all like Jessica's paper dolls: placed neatly in our separate sections in a pleated file. Labeled. I pretended—wished, dreamed—that someday a giant hand would tip the file box upside down, scatter us all from our slots, onto the floor, mixing us together so completely that none of us would know, in the end, who we were, where we belonged, or whether, after all, it even mattered" (*Autumn,* 139).

In a sense, *Autumn Street* is the American version of Lowry's own *Number the Stars*, which also deals with World War II. Both Elizabeth and Annemarie Johansen of *Number the Stars* learn something about the nature of war, although Elizabeth's exposure is more indirect. Like Annemarie, Elizabeth's daily life is also affected by the hostilities, although she never experiences the lack of food or fuel as do the Johansens. Elizabeth's windows, like those of Annemarie, are also covered by blackout curtains. In addition, Elizabeth must wear a dog tag for identification. At the end of both novels, the protagonists face the dangers of the woods, and both children are separated from their best friends. As with Annemarie, the war *has* taken away loved ones, in Elizabeth's case, her father and shell-shocked cousin, David. Unlike Annemarie, however, who eventually confronts the deaths of her Resistance-fighter sister, Lise, and family friend, Peter Neilsen, Elizabeth discovers that death exists outside of war, in the everyday world. Ferdie Gossett, we are told rather specifically, was not mentally maimed during a previous war; rather, his wounds have come from everyday life in the United States.

Before Elizabeth confronts Charles's murder and nearly dies herself, she has already begun to learn about death through stories she hears: Charles tells her about a drunk man named Willard Stanton, who was killed by a train, and her mother relates how Elizabeth's grandmother died in childbirth. Elizabeth comes to fear the death of her own parents, especially her father. Soon death comes much closer to home. Elizabeth blithely helps her sister nudge Japanese beetles into kerosene cans to kill them, then is shocked when a firefly that she captures in her hand also dies. The fragile nature of this insect, which she had hoped to use as a sort of night-light, frightens her. A neighbor boy, Noah Hoffman, who is under psychiatric care, breaks the neck of his cat, Pixie; nearly kills his pet duck, Donald, by dragging him around on a leash; and then dies of pneumonia himself. Innocently, Elizabeth, Charles, and Noah's brother, Nathaniel, ignore Noah's cries for help when he is left alone because they do not like him and do not feel responsible for him. The following day, when Noah dies, Elizabeth briefly believes that she and her friends helped kill him. This particular event stuns Elizabeth, who had accepted Charles's assertion that children do not die. Soon, Elizabeth's own grandfather suffers a stroke that destroys much of what he once was. He can no longer create "magic" by sprinkling special sand over the fire, and he now becomes the child his second wife never had. In order to keep him alive, Elizabeth attempts to communicate with him in small ways, secretly putting cinnamon on his tongue since he cannot do it himself.

Elizabeth, who has temporarily lost both her father and her grandfather, must now face a greater, more permanent, loss. Throughout the tale, she has frequently encountered Ferdie Gossett, a pathetic figure who seems to embody all her fears. Now, when she and Charles finally make their long-awaited trip to the woods at the end of Autumn Street, she returns alone, unable to force the headstrong Charles to come with her. Afterward, Charles is brutally murdered there by Gossett. Elizabeth herself does not come away from the woods unscathed; she is very ill and, as Tatie notes, is also in danger of dying.

When Elizabeth begins to recover, it is her long-absent father, just returned from the war, who comforts her, suggesting that "Bad things won't happen anymore" (*Autumn,* 182). Elizabeth, who has been initiated into the painful realities of the real world, is willing to believe him, recognizing the need for an occasional fiction to sustain hope. "But there are times—times of anguish," the novel concludes, "when an impossible promise to someone you love is as sweet as a cinnamon-smudged fingertip, as nourishing and necessary as the sunlight that comes, still, to consecrate Autumn Street in summer" (*Autumn,* 188). Of Lowry's early works, *Autumn Street* is clearly the most powerful and poetic. Perhaps because the book is so autobiographical, the characters are more fully realized than those in *A Summer to Die* and *Find a Stranger, Say Goodbye.* Autumn Street is clearly a real place, one that, despite the dangers that lurk there, draws the reader in, communicating Lowry's love for the people that, in her memory, still live there.

Not surprisingly, several early reviews of *Autumn Street* raised the question of audience. In particular, one reviewer writes that the novel's "real trouble lies in the question: What age child will read this book?"[15] *The School Library Journal* argued that the book is for "mature readers" who will "be rewarded by a reading experience that touches the heart."[16] *The New Yorker* ignored the question of audience altogether, treating *Autumn Street* as a book for adults, praising it as "dreamlike in remembered feeling" and calling it "a fine novel about the twilight zone between early childhood and the first dawn of adult understanding."[17] Several reviewers, including Barbara Elleman, found the book "emotionally charged," "understandable and unforgettable," although the *Horn Book* suggested that its style was overwrought and several scenes melodramatic.[18] The question of the novel's audience did not deter the American Library Association from awarding it a Notable Book Citation in 1980 or the International Board on Books for Young People from naming it to its 1982 Honor List.

Like many of Lowry's articles and stories and like both *A Summer to Die* and *Find a Stranger, Say Goodbye, Autumn Street* reflects Lowry's interest in the past. Lowry's early work frequently returns to the past—to "Autumn Street"—through a variety of pathways. Although scenes and situations of an earlier era will permeate many of Lowry's books, her next novels, especially those about Anastasia, are more concerned with contemporary life and creating memories in the here and now.

Chapter Three
Anastasia, Poet and Philosopher

When Lowry first began writing a short story about a 10-year-old list-making Bostonian girl with a poet/English professor father and an artist mother, she had no idea that the protagonist would eventually appear in nine children's books and be a secondary character in three more about her younger brother. Since the author's first two novels had been serious in tone and another, *Autumn Street,* which she was writing at the same time, ended with the murder of the protagonist's best friend, creating the story was comic relief. Lowry had, of course, already demonstrated a sense of humor in some of her freelance articles, as when she poked fun at her own experience losing the final round on *Jeopardy*. As she developed Anastasia Krupnik and her family, however, Lowry fell in love with them, prompting her to turn her original short story into a novel, thus launching the career of one of the most popular young heroines in contemporary American children's fiction.

Although Anastasia Krupnik was partly inspired by Lowry's own two daughters and by President Jimmy Carter's daughter, Amy, she also provides a means of wish-fulfillment for Lowry herself. A shy child who did not like rules, young Lois nevertheless would not have stood up to the adults in her life the way that Anastasia does. Comparing herself to Anastasia, Lowry relates, "I was like her when I was growing up in the way that I thought. I had the same kinds of thoughts that she had very often. Rotten thoughts. But I was unlike her in that I didn't ever dare to express them" ("Trumpet I"). Some of Anastasia's feeling toward her much younger brother, Sam, draws on Lowry's own relationship with her older sister, Helen, and her younger brother, Jon. Lowry suggests that she probably has more in common with Anastasia's mother, Katherine Krupnik (another nurturing artist-figure like Will Banks in *A Summer to Die* and Tallie in *Find a Stranger, Say Goodbye*), a character who, like Lowry herself, is described as having a visual imagination. Anastasia's father, Myron Krupnik, Lowry explains, "is sort of my fantasy of who would be a great husband, someone who is intellectual and sweet and smart" (Chaston 1994).

Anastasia Krupnik is also closely related to a long line of young girls in juvenile fiction who are imaginative, witty, insecure, and occasionally impertinent. In Anastasia, there is a little bit of Francis Hodgson Burnett's Mary Lennox (*The Secret Garden* 1911), Louisa May Alcott's Jo March (*Little Women* 1868), Lucy Maud Montgomery's Anne Shirley (*Anne of Green Gables* 1908), and Lowry's favorite comic book character, "Little Lulu." As early reviewers noted, Anastasia bears some resemblance to contemporary fictional heroines such as Louise Fitzhugh's feisty Harriet Welch in *Harriet the Spy* (1964) and Beverly Cleary's beloved pest, Ramona Quimby, in *Ramona, the Pest* (1968) and its sequels. According to Eric Kimmel, "What distinguishes Anastasia from a host of Ellen Conford/Patricia Reilly Giff/Jamie Gibson/Paula Danziger creations is her phenomenal sense of self. Anastasia, like Ozymandias, stands alone, self-assured, confident in her capabilities and judgments, never worrying too much about what others might think."[1]

Nevertheless, Anastasia's sense of self is constantly under siege, and she maintains it only through continual soul-searching. Nor is tragedy far away, despite the comedy inherent in Anastasia's adventures. Kimmel declares that "No writer in the field of children's literature wears both tragic and comic masks as well as Lois Lowry" and that the "roots of Lowry's humor, like Twain's, lie in her constant awareness of life's darker side" (Kimmel, 82). When asked about her humor, Lowry herself remarks, "I don't think I'm a funny person but I see humor in things that other people don't" (Chaston 1994). Thus, although Anastasia agonizes over potential problems such as failed romances, unfeeling teachers, sibling rivalry, moving to a new community, and the death of relatives, the overall tone of the books about her is one of sympathetic humor.

In the first five books of the Anastasia series, Lowry takes her protagonist from the fourth grade into the beginning of seventh grade, establishing an appealing cast of characters who allow her to explore both the joys and trials of early adolescence. As in Lowry's early work, these five books are all concerned with the value of memory, the growth of the imagination, and the disjunction between appearances and reality. These books reveal Lowry's keen sense of humor as well as the close connection between comedy and tragedy.

Anastasia Krupnik (1979)

The first chapter of *Anastasia Krupnik* sets up the contradictions of Anastasia's personality and outlines most of the series' major themes, which provide a tight structure for this seemingly episodic book. As the novel opens, 10-year-old Anastasia is clearly attempting to establish her personal identity. For two years she has unsuccessfully tried to become a professional ice skater and has spent another year training to become a ballerina. As a result, her parents have suggested that she "choose a profession that didn't involve her feet," thus launching her into a search for her own special talents, a pursuit that will culminate in one of the book's sequels, *Anastasia's Chosen Career* (*Anastasia,* 1–2).

In chapter 1 of *Anastasia Krupnik*, Anastasia seems bent on following in her father's footsteps as a writer. She loves poetry, and, when given the opportunity to write a poem for the fourth grade's "Poetry Week," she spends eight days agonizing over it. Carefully choosing each word, she ultimately produces a poem in the style of e. e. cummings. Anastasia's poem about sea creatures is extraordinarily well-written for a child. As she tells her teacher, Mrs. Westvessel, it is "a poem about sounds. . . . It's about little things that live in tidepools, after dark, when they move around. It doesn't have sentences or capital letters because I wanted it to look on the page like small creatures moving in the dark" (*Anastasia,* 12–13). Anastasia clearly has never gotten as much pleasure out of anything as from writing this poem.

Yet, as will happen time and time again in her life, Anastasia's enthusiasm is met with resistance from the pragmatic world in which she lives. Mrs. Westvessel does not appreciate her poem because Anastasia has not followed the rules she has been given. She receives an "F" because she has not used proper punctuation and because her poem does not rhyme. The irony of the situation is that Anastasia, daughter of a real-life poet and whose name appears in the dedication of one of her father's books, is the only member of her class who seems to understand what poetry really is or who might conceivably grow up to become a poet. In response to her teacher's criticism, Anastasia returns home and changes an earlier statement in her notebook about writing a wonderful poem into "I wrote a terrible poem" (*Anastasia,* 14).

As frequently happens in the Anastasia books, however, Anastasia's self-confidence is quickly restored through the help of her close-knit, understanding family. Rather than overreacting, her father reads the poem back to her, making it sound beautiful. He then turns the "F" on top of the poem into the word "Fabulous," prompting Anastasia to return to her notebook and revise her earlier statement to read, "I wrote a fabulous poem" (*Anastasia,* 17). Unfortunately, Anastasia's renewed happiness is very short-lived. When she suddenly realizes that her parents are going to have a new baby, once again she is filled with agony and insecurity.

Anastasia expresses part of her desire to become a writer in the green notebook in which she records her favorite words, important private information, the beginnings of poems, and two lists: "Things I Love!" and "Things I Hate!" These ever changing lists are reproduced at the end of each chapter and serve as a benchmark of Anastasia's growth since she moves items back and forth between them. On the last page only one item, "liver," remains on the list of things that she hates. The contradictory feelings expressed in these lists are reiterated in the titles of the poetry collections Anastasia's father has written: *Laughter Behind the Mask*, *Mystery of Myth*, *Come Morning, Come Night*, and *Bittersweet*. Ironically, later in the novel, one of Dr. Krupnik's poetry students unsuccessfully intellectualizes about "dichotomy," a word that aptly describes both Anastasia's lists and the titles of her father's poetry books.

The novel's first chapter also reveals that Anastasia is introspective, an admirable quality that nevertheless gets her into trouble with others. Highly critical of herself, Anastasia notes that she feels funny because, for the first time in her life, she does not care for her school teacher, nor does she like her elderly grandmother, who lives in a nursing home. In addition, she considers herself dumb because her feelings and tastes differ from those of everyone else. Unlike her friends, she thinks that green ice cream is nauseating, and she is convinced that she is the only person in the world who likes cold spinach sandwiches.

As the novel continues, Anastasia experiences a number of personal, often humorous, crises as a result of trying to establish her individuality. Like Margaret Simon in Judy Blume's *Are You There God, It's Me Margaret* (1970), Anastasia decides to choose a religion for herself. Determining that there are 14 other Catholics in the fourth grade, she decides to become Catholic because she would then belong to a group. She could also get a new name after experiencing First Communion. This appeals to Anastasia because she has never much liked her first name and has no middle name at all. Anastasia thus settles on Catholicism with very little real knowledge of the religion. In the end, however, she changes her mind because she would have to confess her sins and feel sorry for the bad thoughts she has about her teacher. As with Anastasia's conflict with Mrs. Westvessel, Anastasia's parents take her search for religion in stride, allowing her to discover the superficial nature of her decision all on her own.

Nonetheless, Anastasia is still unhappy with her name. None of her friends can spell it, thus, in her mind, preventing them for voting her in as class secretary. "No adult would get caught dead with a name like Anastasia," she mutters to her father (*Anastasia*, 50). In chapter 5, Anastasia finally gains some appreciation for her unusual name, which appropriately symbolizes her own quest for identity. When Anastasia wishes she had a name that ends in the letter *i* so she can join the "i" club like her friends, "Jenni and Becki and Traci and Cindi and Suzi and Luci," Anastasia's father tells her about her namesake, the youngest daughter of the Russian Czar Nicholas II, who was reputedly shot in 1918 (*Anastasia*, 51). When he relates the tale of the woman who for years tried to prove she was actually Anastasia, his daughter's feelings of self-doubt are momentarily dispelled as she fantasizes, "*I could be the real Anastasia!*" (*Anastasia*, 55).

In another chapter, Anastasia tries to establish her identity by attracting the attention of a well-known, sixth-grade individualist, a black boy named Washburn Cummings. Anastasia's notions about romance, however, are shaped by popular culture, in particular by a questionnaire in *Cosmopolitan* magazine that she peruses in the corner drugstore. Once again, Anastasia concludes that the solution to her current problem—how to attract Washburn's attention—is to change herself. As a result, she imitates Washburn by making her own hair stand straight up on top of her head. This new hairstyle, however, merely evokes Washburn's derision, causing her to feel "dumb, dumb, *dumb* again" (*Anastasia*, 47).

As in many of Lowry's books, one of the novel's most prominent themes is the importance of memory. In chapter 6, when her 92-year-old grandmother leaves her nursing home to visit the Krupniks on Thanksgiving, Anastasia is both scared and sad because "Grandmother doesn't remember *anything*" (*Anastasia*, 55). And, indeed, her grandmother does not remember who Anastasia is and thinks her father is still a young man. The only memories that her grandmother has are of the past, and she daydreams that her dead husband, Sam, might come to dinner. "Sam's hands fit around my waist," Anastasia's grandmother tells her, "and do you know, he can pick me right up and swing me around in the air? Sometimes he tickles me on the back of the neck with his mustache" (*Anastasia*, 60). Feeling sorry for her grandmother, Anastasia soon realizes that she does not hate the woman herself, just the fact that she is very old. Appropriately, the favorite plate of her grandmother, who has no short-term memory, is ironically the one with a border of blue "forget-me-nots" (*Anastasia*, 62).

In the very next chapter, Anastasia learns even more about the importance of memory when she visits a class in eighteenth- and nineteenth-century poetry that her father is teaching at Harvard. In preparation for

her visit, Dr. Krupnik has Anastasia read a mimeographed copy of
William Wordsworth's poem, "I Wandered Lonely as a Cloud," and
Anastasia is intrigued by one of its lines, "The inward eye which is the
bliss of solitude" (*Anastasia,* 72).[2] After class, Anastasia's father helps her
to see that the poem suggests that "Memory is the happiness of being
alone." Anastasia concludes, however, that her trouble is that she does
not "have many memories yet" (*Anastasia,* 73). Someday she will need
them to be happy. In response, Anastasia's father suggests that her
grandmother has "the inward eye," that she has memories that allow her
to live in the past, and as a result she is happy.

In chapter 8, Anastasia is further educated about the power of memories as well as the nature of true romance, as her parents share the
unsuccessful romances they had before they were married. Approaching
her mother, Anastasia bemoans the fact that nothing ever happens to
her, which is why she has no memories yet. Her mother counters by
reminding Anastasia of some of the interesting things that *have* happened to her and then describes a memory of her own about an aspiring
stockbroker she once dated. Like Lowry and her own husband, Katherine and the stockbroker had parted company because their fortunes and
future lives did not match.

Later Anastasia talks to her father about creating memories, and he
in turn discloses details of his own frustrated romance with a woman
who ran off to Guatemala and broke his heart. At the end of the chapter, when her grandmother visits at Christmastime, Anastasia asks her
to talk about her husband, Sam. As the old woman talks, she seems to
come back to life. Anastasia realizes that her grandmother has "the
inward eye . . . that makes you feel happy, and not so alone" (*Anastasia,*
84). Anastasia is suddenly sad, however, when her grandmother wants
to go home to be with the deceased Sam.

As the book progresses, Anastasia's feelings toward religion,
romance, and the advent of her brother's birth continue to vacillate, and
she concludes that she has a "mercurial temperament" (*Anastasia,* 87).
She decides to give religion another try, contemplating becoming a Hare
Krishna because, like Catholics, they also get new names. She rekindles
her interest in Washburn Cummings and even feels better about her
new brother, that is, until she learns she cannot be present at his birth.
Having previously been granted the privilege of naming her brother,
Anastasia angrily resolves to name him "One Ball Reilly" after a song
she has overheard but does not quite understand.

In the novel's last two chapters, Anastasia's search for memories and for self-understanding come to a head, and the list of things she hates begins to grow smaller and smaller. Her grandmother dies, and suddenly Anastasia realizes that she is beginning to build up powerful memories of her own. Like the memories that Jonas receives in Lowry's later novel, *The Giver*, not all of them feel good. Anastasia has come to appreciate her grandmother through the reminiscences that she has shared and now mourns her loss. "I have no grandmother all of a sudden," she concludes, writing in her green notebook. "But I have an inward eye for the first time" (*Anastasia,* 100).

The death of Anastasia's grandmother also furnishes her with some insight into her teacher, Mrs. Westvessel, who telephones to comfort her, having recently experienced the death of her own elderly mother. Anastasia removes Mrs. Westvessel's name from the "Things I Hate" list, feeling sorry for wishing her teacher would get pimples. At the same time, Anastasia's baby brother finally arrives, and she discovers that she likes him. Unconsciously perpetuating the recollections that her grandmother has shared with her, she names her brother Sam—after her grandfather. The book ends with the Krupniks together, unified, creating new memories.

Although a few writers found some moments contrived, the initial response to *Anastasia Krupnik* was overwhelmingly positive. Writing in the *Horn Book*, Ann A. Flowers suggests that the story itself is slight but praises the novel's characters. "Anastasia's father and mother," she contends, ". . . are among the most humorous, sensible, and understanding parents to be found in recent fiction, and Anastasia herself is an amusing and engaging heroine."[3] Other reviewers argue that Lowry "masterfully captures the heart and mind of a perceptive fourth grader."[4] Most important, Lowry's young readers immediately began writing her, begging for more stories about the Krupnik family.

Anastasia Again! (1981)

"Oddly enough," Lowry maintains, "when I wrote the first book about Anastasia I had no intention that it become a series. I got so many letters from kids wanting another book about her that I sat down and wrote a second one. And because [Anastasia's] brother had been born on the last page of the first book, I knew he was going to appear in the second book and I figured if he was just a year old he'd be kind of boring, so I made him two years old which meant she had to be twelve" (Chaston 1994).

Anastasia Again! moves forward in time to the end of Anastasia's sixth-grade year. As a result of this jump in time, Lowry occasionally receives letters from children who want to know which book features Anastasia's experiences in fifth grade, the missing year of her life. In some ways, Anastasia's aging helps mitigate criticism that she is unbelievably precocious. Furthermore, *Anastasia Again!* now places Anastasia in a stage in life full of the contradictions and insecurities already reflected in her personality.

In *Anastasia Again!* the Krupnik family has not changed much. Anastasia still exhibits mixed emotions about people and events, her father still makes lists and writes poetry, and her mother still struggles to balance a career as an artist with her domestic responsibilities. Sam, however, is now two and a half years old and, as his mother explains, speaks like Walter Cronkite.

As might be expected in a sequel, *Anastasia Again!* covers some of the same ground as the original book. Once again, Anastasia feels that her parents have unfairly come to a decision without consulting her. As in the first book, Anastasia vacillates in her feelings toward others, struggles to become a writer, and grows to appreciate yet another elderly woman, Gertrude Stein, who becomes the Krupniks' surrogate grandmother for the rest of the series. In addition, the themes of both books include the importance of memory, the value of the elderly, the struggles involved in maintaining friendships, and, most important, the dangers of making what Anastasia's father calls "premature assumptions."[5]

As in *Anastasia Krupnik*, this novel's themes and episodic plot revolve mostly around one major problem. In this case, the Krupniks have decided to move to the suburbs. The melodramatic Anastasia threatens to throw herself out the window (although she is reminded that the family lives on the first floor). Finally, she agrees to move if the family can find a house with a tower bedroom, a requirement that is actually met. The rest of the book concerns Anastasia's adapting to her family's move across the Charles River from Cambridge, where she lives in an apartment much like the one Lowry occupied while her husband was in law school, to a Boston suburb. Although she did not specifically name Anastasia's new neighborhood, Lowry says that she was thinking of Brookline, a Boston suburb that would be close enough to Cambridge for two children to reach by bicycle as they do later in the novel. Brookline also includes several houses with towers much like the one that the Krupniks buy (Chaston 1994).

One of the novel's main themes grows directly out of Anastasia's initial aversion to moving, which is based on the portrayal of suburban life in books, magazines, and television. While in *Anastasia Krupnik*, Anastasia bases her conception of the world on these popular media, it becomes an even greater problem in this novel. In this respect, she resembles a number of other literary characters who mistakenly confuse the real world with the books they read, including the title character of Cervantes's *Don Quixote* (1613–14), Arabella in Charlotte Lennox's *Female Quixote* (1752), and Marianne Dashwood in Jane Austen's *Sense and Sensibility* (1811).[6] Children's novels as varied as Lewis Carroll's *Alice's Adventures in Wonderland* (1865) and E. Nesbit's *Story of the Treasure Seekers* (1899) all feature young readers who discover their literary-based views of the world contradicted during their adventures.[7]

When asked how she knows so much about the suburbs, Anastasia explains, "Books and TV. Mostly TV commercials. You never see *city* people worrying about ring-around-the-collar" (*Again,* 46). As a result of her reading and viewing, Anastasia is convinced that everyone in the suburbs lives in a split-level home with matching furniture, no bookcases, a huge color television, and paint-by-number pictures of mountains or kittens. Early in the book, Anastasia's father loudly warns her about jumping to conclusions about suburbanites: "YOU ARE MAKING HASTY JUDGEMENTS! IDIOTIC PREMATURE ASSUMPTIONS! AND YOU ARE ALSO MAKING ME MISS THE RED SOX GAME ON TV!" (*Again,* 4) Later, after the family has moved, Anastasia's mother echoes this sentiment, reminding her that all of her "premature assumptions" have been disproved.

Anastasia's preconceptions, however, are not limited to suburban life. She also fancies herself an expert both on romance and psychology because she reads *Cosmopolitan* (a magazine her father dubs a waste of money). She plans on reading an article in it on how to make "spritely conversation" with former classmate Robert Giannini. Another article inspires her to diagnose her parents as suffering from "Post-moving depression." *Cosmopolitan* also tells Anastasia that it is fashionable for blonde-haired women not to shave their legs.

Throughout the novel, Anastasia sees her life as a work of literature and, indeed, works on transforming her daily experience into a novel. She imagines she is Rapunzel, letting her hair down to provide a prince entrance into her tower bedroom; decides Gertrude Stein lives in a "Charles Addams" house; and thinks her neighbor, Steve Harvey, looks like Luke Skywalker from *Star Wars*. When her father says that Gertrude Stein, her new neighbor, is supposed to be dead, Anastasia does not realize that he is referring to the famous American writer of the same name and thinks, "I'm living in a ghost story" (*Again*, 66).

Some of Anastasia's preconceived ideas are merely a result of her inclination to overdramatize and exaggerate events. For example, she jumps to the conclusion that she will have to marry Robert Giannini because he "loves" her and she will never find anyone else who will. Anastasia also imagines that "Dear Abby" would laugh at her problems if she wrote her a letter asking for advice.

Although Anastasia's brother is also prone to making prejudgments, this is quite understandable for a two-year-old. Because Gertrude Stein is old and unkempt, Sam announces that a witch lives next door, and he quickly turns her name into "Gertrustein," recalling the monster in Mary Shelley's "Frankenstein." Nor is Anastasia's mother guiltless. She all too quickly assumes that the people Anastasia invites to her party are teenagers and not members of a Senior Citizen Center. Katherine Krupnik also confides to Anastasia that a man she once dated thought she was the daughter of a well-known impressionist painter, Franz Kline, and she even failed a college exam so he would not discover his mistake. Even Anastasia's friends are guilty of jumping to conclusions. When Anastasia misuses her favorite word, *weird*, Robert Giannini erroneously assumes that Sam must be retarded. (Later, in a humorous scene, Anastasia's father tries to get her to use one of a number of synonyms instead of always saying "weird.") Steve Harvey thinks that people from Cambridge are intellectual snobs.

Eventually, Anastasia recognizes the false nature of her illusions. For example, she quickly decides that a prince would slide down her greasy hair if she tried to act like Rapunzel. The houses in the suburbs, she discovers, are not all alike. Gertrude Stein is actually shy and not a monster. At the end of the book, when Steve reveals his own preconceptions about Cambridge, Anastasia finally learns her lesson. Steve explains that until he met Anastasia, he thought that people from Cambridge "were all intellectuals who sat around in the evenings drinking rose hip tea and playing recorders" (*Again*, 126).

One of the ways in which the various characters form premature assumptions is through language, and, as usual, the novel is filled with wordplay. Gertrude Stein reveals that she was put off by her former husband's insistence that a double "l" should be pronounced as a "y" and that she call him "Yoyd" and not "Lloyd." Lowry herself plays with names, calling Anastasia's neighbor after the Bohemian writer, Gertrude Stein, making Sam think of "Frankenstein." (Similarly, the name of Anastasia's athletic boyfriend, Steve Harvey, conjures up Steve Garvey, the once popular professional baseball player.)

While Anastasia is learning her lesson about preconceptions, the novel also suggests the value of both history and memory, main themes of the first book. Largely because of the memories she has about her home, Anastasia does not want to move: "The whole apartment had a history, and it was *her* history and her parents' history and beginning to be Sam's" (*Again,* 5). This is a feeling Anastasia shares with the other members of her family. Her mother is nostalgic about the stained glass windows in some cupboards, her father signs his name on the wallpaper near his desk, and Sam, with Anastasia's help, leaves half of his blanket behind, hidden in the back of a cupboard. Anastasia herself misses the wallpaper in her room, and her mother promises to find more of the same pattern for her new bedroom.

Losing oneself in memories, however, can also create problems. Gertrude Stein has isolated herself since her husband ran off, and, despite the fact that Gertrude is 80-odd years old, Anastasia has to help her look toward her future and make friends with other people. At the end of the second chapter in the novel she is writing, Anastasia explains that "her Past began to catch up with her, and to get tangled up with her Future" (*Again,* 106).

As is the case in several of the later Anastasia books, the novel ends with a party in which the characters come together and resolve their differences. Anastasia, Steve Harvey, Robert Giannini, Jenny MacCauley, Gertrude Stein, and the members of the Senior Citizen Center all become friends, and what is almost a major catastrophe is transformed into a happy ending, Anastasia's past and future coming together harmoniously.

One way for Anastasia to preserve her memories, she discovers, is through her own writing. In *Anastasia Again!* Anastasia has moved from recording her thoughts and emotions in a number of lists (and one poem) to writing a mystery, since she believes that Nancy Drew books have no relationship to real life. After all, she asks, whose real life includes "haunted houses, spiral staircases, or twisted candlesticks? Yet real life—especially Anastasia's real life—was full of mysteries" (*Again,* 8). At the end of each chapter of *Anastasia Again!* we find Anastasia exploring these puzzles by writing an unintentionally comical novel inspired by her own life.

Anastasia begins her writing project by trying to find an appropriate title, testing such possibilities as "The Mystery of Why Some People Make Decisions without Consulting Their Twelve-Year-Old Children," "The Mystery of the Girl Who Lived in a Tower," "The Mystery . . . of Why Other People Think Your Very Serious Problems are Hysterically Funny," and "The Mystery . . . of Why You Sometimes Hate the Idea of Something, but Then You Like the Thing Itself" (*Again,* 9, 20, 34, 41). She finally comes up with "The Mystery . . . of Saying Good-by" (*Again,* 51). She then begins to write her book, mixing the mystery conventions of one of her favorite writers, Agatha Christie, with elements of her own life. For example, when she decides that in Agatha Christie books there is at least one murder by chapter 4, Anastasia throws in the line, "Mozart was dead" (*Again,* 128). At the end of the novel, deciding her book needs to be spiced up, she includes what she calls "explicit sex," writing, "The naked man had a poking out bellybutton. And Mozart was still dead" (*Again,* 145).

The second half of *Anastasia Again!* anticipates Anastasia's romantic mishaps in later books. She worries about what her nemesis, Robert Giannini, will think of what she is wearing when he asks her to go bike riding, and she is angry later when, in her absence, he takes her former best friend, Jenny MacCauley, to see *Casablanca.* As already mentioned, Anastasia decides she may have to marry Robert someday. Then, after a conversation with her mother, Anastasia momentarily considers whether she will get married at all. With the introduction of Steve Harvey into the series, Anastasia gains a boyfriend and immediately tries to use him to make Robert jealous. In contrast to Anastasia's own budding romances, Lowry contrasts the disastrous marriage of Gertrude Stein and her former husband with the warm, comfortable relationship between Myron and Katherine Krupnik.

Anastasia Again! clearly sets the tone for the rest of the series. Unlike *Anastasia Krupnik,* it focuses on a shorter period of time and one major dilemma, as opposed to a year in Anastasia's life that is climaxed by both a birth and a death. Featured as characters in two books, the Krupnik family began to gain more widespread critical attention, including a review in the *New York Times,* which, however, suggested that the book was a disappointment and that the Krupniks had slipped "into sounding clever without always having something to say."[8] This criticism notwithstanding, other reviewers praised the sequel.[9] Indeed, Mary M. Burns

went as far as to dub Anastasia "one of the most intriguing female protagonists to appear in children's books since the advent of Harriet the
Spy nearly two decades ago" (Burns 1981, 535). *Anastasia Again!* won
the Anastasia series its first major award, a 1983 American Book Award
Nomination in the juvenile paperback category.

Anastasia at Your Service (1982)

Lowry's third book about Anastasia, *Anastasia at Your Service*, continues
where *Anastasia Again!* left off. It is the only book in the series in which
some form of Anastasia's own writing is not presented at the end of
most chapters. As in *Anastasia Again!* 12-year-old Anastasia learns that
judging people by surface appearances is dangerous, although the book
specifically focuses on class snobbery.

The novel finds the often overly dramatic Anastasia claiming that she
is suffering from "severe depression," "boredom," and "poverty," ostensi-
bly because she is still a newcomer in her neighborhood and has made
few friends.[10] The beginning of her seventh-grade year is still nearly a
month away. Ever ready to provide solutions to other people's problems,
Anastasia's father suggests that Anastasia get a job.

Still a romantic, the well-read Anastasia continues to view the world
through books. In the first chapter, Anastasia has been acting out the
deathbed scenes from books she has read, including *Little Women*, *Romeo
and Juliet*, and *Charlotte's Web*. When she contemplates getting a job, she
decides to become a companion to a rich woman, as in the mystery novels
of Mary Roberts Rinehart. In the two-page advertisement that she places
around town, Anastasia announces that she wants to read "aloud to her
employer . . . Gothic novels and stuff," and after each chapter they can
"discuss romance and give each other advice about love if either one of
them has an admirer" (*Service*, 15). The title of her flyer, "Anastasia Atcher
Service," comes from Sam's mispronunciation of Anastasia's motto, which
she imagines might be the future name of a worldwide corporation.[11]

When one of the town's truly wealthy women, Mrs. Ferris Bellingham, calls and offers her a job at her home, "Bellmeadow Farm," Anastasia assumes that her fantasy has come true. After all, Mrs. Bellingham
lives in an "immense stone house, so large it looked like a school or hospital" with "a long curving driveway with trees" and two "black cars like
presidential limousines" (*Service*, 22). Anastasia imagines being adopted
like the heroine of *Rebecca of Sunnybrook Farm* (a book she hates) and discussing *Gone with the Wind* with Mrs. Bellingham's friends.

Anastasia is taken aback, however, when she is assigned to polish silver. Gradually she realizes that Mrs. Bellingham only wants some additional cheap domestic help. Furious because she feels that Mrs. Bellingham has tricked her, Anastasia decides to quit but cannot because her employer insists that she work to pay the $35 to replace a silver spoon that she accidentally bent in the garbage disposal. This sets up the novel's basic plot: Anastasia's conflict with Mrs. Bellingham. The following day Anastasia is forced to serve as a maid at a luncheon Mrs. Bellingham is giving for her granddaughter, Daphne. Anastasia finds this especially embarrassing since Daphne is also beginning the seventh grade. Uncharacteristically, Anastasia bursts into tears at the dinner table as she reveals this new dilemma to her parents, prompting them to share some of their own awkward moments.

Anastasia's popularity with young readers probably stems from the fact that she generally tries to do something about her problems, even though the results are often disastrous. This time she disguises herself as a middle-aged woman at the luncheon so that Daphne will not know they are the same age. To accomplish this, Anastasia stuffs her mother's bra with pantyhose and puts Johnson's baby powder on her hair. No one at the luncheon, however, even notices her disguise, with the exception of Daphne, who sees Anastasia accidentally dip her pantyhose-filled breasts into a platter of deviled eggs. Daphne rescues her from this further humiliation by spilling Coke on her own dress and asking Anastasia to help her clean it. Thus begins a friendship that continues throughout the series.

Daphne, it turns out, makes the sometimes eccentric Anastasia appear quite ordinary by comparison. Because her father is a Congregational minister and her parents are too nice and always forgiving, Daphne has set out to become a juvenile delinquent. She smokes, paints her room black, even mows a swastika into her front lawn, although these rebellious acts are only an attempt at attracting her parent's attention. Daphne also dislikes her grandmother because of her occasional bigoted remarks about the poor and because she gave her a doll for her 13th birthday. Together, Daphne and Anastasia decide to take revenge on Daphne's grandmother. Mrs. Bellingham is giving a big party, and the girls plan on sending invitations to "all the so-called undesirable people in this town," including a drunk, a bag lady, a former drug pusher, and people from low-income housing (*Service,* 70).

Once again, Anastasia's humorous problems are tempered by a serious situation. This time, Anastasia's brother, Sam, falls from his bedroom window, fractures his skull, and ends up in the hospital. This prompts a moment of real fear for Anastasia, who fantasizes that she would do practically anything (including eating raw liver, marrying the revolting Robert Giannini, having her nose amputated, joining the Ku Klux Klan, and standing naked in the window of Lord and Taylor's department store without a ski mask) in order to keep Sam from dying. This experience helps Anastasia realize how much she cares for her own family and that Daphne is missing something with hers.

Sam's adventures in the hospital also give him a chance to once again show off his precocious nature. For example, he entertains the hospital staff with songs that would be more appropriate coming from a fraternity member than a two-year-old. He returns home with a bald head (which Mrs. Krupnik says makes him look like Kojak) and stories of a kindly woman named "Mrs. Flypaper," an apparently imaginary friend who has given him advice on getting well. She has even convinced him to eat soft-boiled eggs, something he always thought he hated.

At the same time, Anastasia has another experience that helps her further appreciate her family. Misinterpreting Anastasia's use of the phrase, "the great unwashed," her parents assume that she has taken on some of Mrs. Bellingham's snobbery, and they set out to teach her about her own heritage. Anastasia's father takes her to see the neighborhood where, as the son of poor immigrants from Czechoslovakia, he grew up. Anastasia decides she loves this part of town, which gives her a homey, friendly feeling.

Both Anastasia's experiences with Mrs. Bellingham and her grand-daughter as well as Sam's sojourn in the hospital lead to the novel's climax, in which Anastasia again learns about the deceptive nature of surface appearances. Anastasia and Daphne's plan to take revenge on Mrs. Bellingham backfires. It turns out that Mrs. Bellingham's big party is a fund-raiser for the pediatric ward of the hospital where Sam had stayed after his accident. When Anastasia and Daphne try to defuse their plan by uninviting the "undesirables" from the party, they cannot tell them apart from the rich people who are supposed to be there. Anastasia nearly mistakes the doctor who operated on Sam for the drunk they invited, while Daphne tells the mayor that she thinks that he is "a dein-stitutionalized psychotic" (*Service,* 138). In the end, Daphne and Anastasia explain everything to Mrs. Bellingham, who is surprisingly calm about the situation but who is hurt by the fact that the girls have been afraid of her. When Anastasia, accompanied by Sam, returns to Bellmeadow Farm finally to get paid, Sam reveals that Mrs. Bellingham is his friend, "Mrs. Flypaper," the kindly hospital volunteer whom he has grown to love.

Like Mrs. Bellingham, Daphne, too, reveals another side to her personality: She really does want to do well in school and to change her relationship with her parents. Because she is tired of black, she even contemplates painting her room yellow. Daphne's parents also prove they love her by finally expressing concern about her actions. The novel ends with Anastasia and Daphne vowing to help each other out as school starts.

Like the other books in this series, *Anastasia at Your Service* is filled with literary allusions. Besides references to the books Anastasia has read, the novel features a scene appreciated only by adult readers in which Anastasia dusts the volumes in Mrs. Bellingham's library. As she peruses Mrs. Bellingham's books, she recognizes a number of authors' names because her father has mentioned them. She is surprised, however, that Henry James has written more books than the author of the Nancy Drew series. She also imagines that the great writer is still alive but that he is probably so busy writing books that he has never ordered pizza or been to a disco. Perhaps, Anastasia muses, her father could acquaint Mrs. Bellingham with the plots of James's books, and they could invite him to dinner, thus precipitating a big romance. This scene, although paying humorous homage to great writers such as Henry James, F. Scott Fitzgerald, and Willa Cather clearly shows their lack of importance to a well-read, 12-year-old who gains sustenance from children's books and popular fiction.

Anastasia at Your Service elicited much the same sort of response from reviewers as the two books that preceded it. Zena Sutherland praises the book, suggesting that it was written with the same wit and polish as the other books but that it is not quite as substantial structurally.[12] Once again, Ann A. Flowers extols the merits of Myron and Katherine Krupnik, suggesting that Anastasia is the "fortunate possessor of the most sensible, sympathetic, cheerful, and amusing parents in children's literature."[13] Writing in *Language Arts,* Ruth M. Stein argues that this book is her favorite in the series and that its precise "character delineation, dialogue that's right on the nose, and the element of authentic craziness raise Anastasia to Harriet and Ramona's level."[14]

Anastasia, Ask Your Analyst (1984)

Anastasia, Ask Your Analyst, like most of the later books in the series, takes place during Anastasia's seventh-grade year. Like *Anastasia on Her*

Own, it focuses on Anastasia's relationships with her parents, now that she is 13 and suddenly discovers their faults. Both of these books are less complex and less thematically rich than the first three Anastasia books; on the other hand, they contain some of the most humorous scenes in the series.

Lowry explores Anastasia's angst at becoming 13 through three main story lines: her changing attitudes toward her parents, her science project involving two pet gerbils, and her brother's problems with a young bully named Nicky Coletti. At least two of these plots were inspired by one of Lowry's readers since her dedication reads, "For the child in Nebraska who wrote and suggested that the Krupniks should have pets, and Sam should have a friend."[15] At the beginning of *Anastasia, Ask Your Analyst*, Anastasia, who has recently turned 13, decides that her understanding and supportive parents are actually "weird" and embarrassing. This is a common malady of all 13-year-olds, her mother assures her: "I bet anything that in Alaska, thirteen-year-old Eskimo girls get together and talk about how weird their mothers are. In China. Africa. Everywhere." "When people begin to mature physically," she comforts Anastasia, "all those hormones start rushing around, or something," causing them to dislike their parents (*Analyst,* 23).

Eventually, Anastasia decides that maybe her family is not as weird as she thought. Perhaps Anastasia herself is the one with an abnormal personality. Maybe *she* needs psychiatric help. Anastasia has seen *Sybil*, a television movie about a woman with multiple personalities and soon decides she has the same problem. "I have all these different personalities seething inside me!" Anastasia exclaims (*Analyst,* 40).

Anastasia's father, however, refuses to let her visit a psychiatrist. "[B]asically you are a very nice, very bright thirteen-year-old who is experiencing normal difficulty adjusting to adolescence," he tells her (*Analyst,* 40). Trying to understand parent/teenager relationships more clearly, Anastasia consults her friends, Meredith Halberg and Sonya Isaacson, who are facing similar difficulties with their parents. Sonya responds that her own father, like Anastasia's mother, blames her problems on hormones.

Anastasia's wish to consult a psychiatrist ends when she buys a plaster bust of Sigmund Freud at a garage sale. The bust serves as a sounding board for Anastasia, who begins telling it all of her problems. These include Daphne Bellingham's defection from her group of girlfriends to chase boys, her parents' annoying and upsetting behavior, Sam's harassment by a nursery school bully, and her science project, which starts getting out of hand.

Like Anastasia, Sam is also coping with a new problem. One day he comes home from nursery school complaining about a classmate named Nicky, who bites. Anastasia comes to his rescue, providing her parents with a possible way to help her brother. She suggests that her mother invite Nicky over to play. "Make sure that you invite Mrs. Coletti, too, so that she doesn't just drop Nicky off. You want her to stay, so that she can *see* Nicky beating up on poor Sam. She'll be a witness, and she won't think you're making it up" (*Analyst,* 84). Anastasia's mother calls her a genius—until the Colettis arrive. Mrs. Coletti is a self-righteous snob, passing judgment on everything about the Krupniks, from Sam's toys to the heating system in the house to the fact that Anastasia's mother works. Meanwhile, Nicky, who turns out to be a girl, wreaks havoc on the Krupnik's house while Mrs. Coletti watches, blithely chalking up her daughter's behavior to hyperactivity.

While visiting the Krupniks, Nicky lets loose the gerbils Anastasia has been keeping as part of her school science project. Early in the book, against the wishes of her mother, who claims that she has "rodent phobia," Anastasia decides to keep two gerbils, Romeo and Juliet, to study their mating habits. Throughout the novel, the report Anastasia writes about the gerbils is reproduced. The account frequently wanders away from its subject, however, and is filled with Anastasia's own self-psychoanalysis.

Like Nicky Coletti, Romeo turns out to be a female. In fact, both gerbils are pregnant, giving birth to nine babies between them, a fact that Anastasia hides from her mother. As always preoccupied with names, Anastasia allows Sam to decide what to call the baby gerbils. He chooses "Happy," "Sneezy," "Bashful," "Doc," "Grumpy," "Sleepy," "Dopey," "Snow White," and "Prince." After the gerbils escape, Anastasia and Sam eventually recapture them but not before their father concludes that the house is filled with poltergeists when he catches brief glimpses of the animals. Eventually their mother finds out that the gerbils have multiplied, and the Krupniks decide to give them to the Colettis as a "present" since Nicky has broken both legs. When her mother feels guilty about taking revenge on the obnoxious Colettis, Anastasia offers to lend her the bust of Sigmund Freud. At the end of the novel, Anastasia does not mind her parents anymore; they no longer seem weird. Her hormones, she announces, are gone.

Although *Anastasia, Ask Your Analyst* lacks some of the pathos and depth of the other installments in the series, it develops Anastasia's relationship with her mother and captures the essence of becoming 13 years old. The book does include two autobiographical elements. Before Lowry began writing on a computer, she used to keep her manuscripts in the refrigerator to protect them, as Anastasia's father does in this novel. Myron Krupnik has also been a nominee for an American Book Award, as was Lowry for *Anastasia Again!*

Although praising the book's humor and wit, two reviewers also criticized it. Kate M. Flanagan suggests that Lowry's repetition of Anastasia's previous journal entries, each time she writes a new one, is tiresome. She also attacks "the author's inclusion of several references to ethnic groups and to the handicapped which might well be disturbing to some people," ultimately making the Krupniks "just a little less likable than before."[16] Carolyn Noah suggests that one basic problem with this novel is the ending. Anastasia has been complaining about her hormones throughout the book and then, rather too conveniently, "declares that all her 'hormones' are gone, along with all her other problems." According to Noah, we have come "to expect more effective character resolution from this author."[17] Such criticisms notwithstanding, the book received the 1986 Garden State Children's Book Award from the New Jersey Library Association and was named one of *Booklist*'s Best Books for Children in 1984.

Anastasia on Her Own (1985)

For *Anastasia on Her Own*, Lowry borrows a plot that has its roots in the oral tradition and that has been popularized in a number of children's books, films, and television series. At the beginning of this novel, Anastasia and her father do not appreciate the strain Katherine Krupnik feels from balancing dual careers as an artist and a homemaker. In an effort to help Katherine out, they provide her with a schedule to help her become more organized. Shortly afterward, however, Anastasia and her father are forced to assume Katherine's domestic responsibilities, creating havoc in their home.

Husbands who trade roles with their wives have, of course, been the subject of stories for centuries. One of the most well known, "The Husband Who Was to Mind the House," was retold by Peter Asbjörnsen in his collection of Scandinavian folktales and features a husband who ends up in the chimney after trying to feed a cow on the roof of his thatched cottage.[18] Similarly, inept husbands, at least initially unable to handle domestic chores, have appeared in television situation comedies such as *I Love Lucy* (1951–61) and films such as *Mr. Mom* (1983). An early review of *Anastasia on Her Own* compares the book to a another novel about domestic difficulties, Betty MacDonald's *The Egg and I* (1945).

In books for the young, children, too, are often forced to take on domestic responsibilities, learning to appreciate their parents (usually their mothers). A good example of this appears in Louisa May Alcott's influential novel, *Little Women* (1868), a work that Anastasia herself alludes to in *Anastasia at Your Service*. In one chapter of Alcott's novel, Marmee effectively goes on strike, leaving the girls to take care of the household chores. When things go wrong, the girls recognize the importance of each family member's cooperation. "Don't you feel that it is pleasanter to help one another," Marmee asks her daughters, "to have daily duties which make leisure sweet when it comes, and to bear or forebear, that home may be comfortable and lovely to us all?"[19] Contemporary variations of this same situation include Mary Rodger's *Freaky Friday* (1972), in which Anabelle Andrews turns into her mother for a day, making a mess of household duties; and the popular film, *Home Alone* (1990), in which Kevin McCallister fends for himself when his family accidentally leaves him at their Chicago home while they travel to France for Christmas.

When Katherine Krupnik rather unashamedly admits that she is the world's worst housekeeper, Anastasia and Myron both conclude that her problems can be solved if she becomes more organized. Together they create a schedule for completing household chores, which appears in frequently modified versions throughout the text, much like Anastasia's lists of things she hates and loves in *Anastasia Krupnik*, her mystery novel in *Anastasia Again!*, and her report in *Anastasia, Ask Your Analyst*. The first household schedule does not work because it is inflexible and does not account for emergencies such as a problematic furnace, a flat tire for the driver of Sam's carpool, Sam's accidentally shoplifting a pack of Dentyne gum, and a pair of black socks that discolors a load of white laundry.

When Anastasia's mother has to go to Los Angeles for 10 days to serve as an advisor for an animated film version of a picture book she has illustrated, Anastasia and her father get to put their list-making ability to the test. The result of course is complete chaos. To begin with, Sam almost immediately comes down with chicken pox. Then, as in a later book in the series, *Anastasia at This Address*, Anastasia suddenly becomes enamored with the idea of romance. Soon she finds herself making dinner for the boy of her dreams, Steve Harvey, and her father's old girl-friend, Annie O'Donnell, who has inconveniently swept into town. Once again, Anastasia consults *Cosmopolitan* for help, adhering to the guidelines in an article entitled, "Creating a Romantic Evening." Since the article suggests that her dinner have a color scheme and identifies purple as the color of passion, Anastasia dyes the tablecloth purple. She also assumes that she can cook a gourmet dinner merely by following recipes in *Mastering the Art of French Cooking* and soon makes a mess of "Ragout de Veau aux Champignons."

The dinner is a disaster—anything but passionate. With advice from a man on the phone who is peddling tap-dancing lessons, Anastasia uses panty hose instead of cheesecloth to help cook the veal, then neglects to remove the veal marrow and knucklebones before serving it, which upsets Annie. In preparing the meal, Anastasia also transforms the kitchen into a disaster area. Along the way, she inadvertently dyes her own arms purple and has to wear long gloves. The guests themselves are obnoxious: Annie O'Donnell is an enormous woman with frizzy red curls, eyelashes like spikes, and monstrous earrings, who criticizes every-one else's looks, while Steve Harvey is definitely not interested in Anas-tasia, only food. At the conclusion of the evening, Myron Krupnik, who has been uncomfortable about meeting Annie, succumbs to Sam's chicken pox. Her pride broken, Anastasia finally calls her mother for help. With Katherine's return, order is restored. The housekeeping schedules are cheerfully torn up; Anastasia's mother uses her earnings to buy a microwave. The novel concludes, "And it sure felt good, having her mother back in charge."[20]

Somewhat more predictable and less complex, *Anastasia on Her Own* does carry forward several motifs from previous books in the series. Anastasia is still grappling with defining herself, which is not helped by the fact that Steve Harvey continues to create new nicknames for her from various subjects they are studying at school. Anastasia, who has never liked her name, fights off new appellations such as "Anapestic," "Anaconda," "Anachronism," and "Analgesia." This last word, which Anastasia discovers from her dictionary means "insensitive to pain," is ironic. Despite the humor of her situation, Anastasia realizes that she "was so sensitive to pain that she had been suffering the entire evening, and not just from the horrible earrings. And she was *still* suffering" (*Own*, 120). Although Anastasia does not grow much in this book, she certainly comes to value her mother, recognizing that she herself is not completely ready to assume adult roles.

Lowry admits that some young readers have written to her attacking the silly behavior of the generally lovable Myron Krupnik in this book, a criticism she now accepts as valid (Chaston 1994). When originally published, *The Bulletin of the Center for Children's Books* suggested that *Anastasia on Her Own* does not have a strong story line. On the other hand, Ann A. Flowers calls it "the best sequel yet," contending that "Lois Lowry is fast becoming the Beverly Cleary for the upper middle grades," and Laura Zaidman praises its "witty, realistic characterization."[21]

Although *Anastasia, Ask Your Analyst* and *Anastasia on Her Own* are less complicated than their three predecessors, they are humorous, enjoyable works that have helped further establish the popularity of the series. As of the moment, they have been followed by four more books about Anastasia and three about Sam. Most of the later works adopt the streamlined plots and narrow focus established in *Anastasia, Ask Your Analyst* and *Anastasia on Your Own* while returning to some of the thematic complexity of the first two books in the series.

Chapter Four

The Amazing Krupniks

In 1984, after completing her fourth book about Anastasia, Lowry told *Contemporary Authors*, "I have the feeling that she's going to go on for-ever—or until I get quite sick of her, which hasn't happened yet. I'm still very fond of her and her whole family" (Ross, 334). After complet-ing five more books about Anastasia and three more about her brother, Sam, Lowry says she intends to write more about both of them. Since she has determined that Anastasia will not get much older, Lowry must carefully coordinate events in each new book with those in the rest of the series. In an interview with Mickey Pearlman, Lowry explains that her "psyche requires amusement from time to time, and the 'Anastasia' books provide that. They are very easy to write because I know all the characters, I know where the books are set, I know where Anastasia lives, and I know her friends. . . . So when I just need to relax and tee-hee a little to myself, I say, 'It's time to write another book about Anas-tasia' " (Pearlman, 173).

By now, Anastasia has had one of the longest and busiest seventh-grade years in history. Nevertheless, the Krupniks seem every bit as lively as in the first books. There seems to be no end to the difficulties into which Anastasia and her amazing family manage to land. Indeed, the later books in the series, as well as the Sam books, contain some of Lowry's most humorous and appealing work, once again focusing largely on Anastasia's and Sam's searches for personal identity and the support they receive from those around them. In the last four books in the series, *Anastasia Has the Answers, Anastasia's Chosen Career, Anastasia at This Address*, and *Anastasia, Absolutely*, Anastasia struggles harder than ever to establish her individuality and attempts to complete many of the developmental tasks that Robert J. Havinghurst suggests that young adults experience: achieving gender roles, accepting one's appear-ance, establishing emotional independence from one's parents, selecting an occupation, and developing relationships with the opposite sex.[1] The three books about Anastasia's brother are also about creating a sense of self, as Sam moves from infancy into childhood.

Anastasia Has the Answers (1986)

Anastasia Has the Answers returns to some of the major themes of the
first Anastasia book: the trials of public school life, the need to succeed,
love and infatuation, and death and grief. Anastasia also continues her
education in the true nature of romance and, through a friend, confronts
the difficulties that occur when parents divorce. Once again, these topics
are tied to one of Anastasia's problems, one that might seem fairly simple: She cannot climb the rope in her gym class. Moreover, her class is to
demonstrate rope climbing for a visiting team of foreign educators.

The gym teacher, Ms. Willoughby, who recognizes Anastasia's difficulties with the rope, puts her in charge of blowing the whistle. This
offends Anastasia, who has previously taken solace in Ms. Willoughby's
belief that she will someday be able to climb it. "One of these days you'll
amaze yourself," Ms. Willoughby tells her. "You'll leap up there and
you'll just keep going, all the way to the ceiling."[2] In a sort of parody of
countless sports novels and films in which practice turns losers into
champions, Anastasia learns how to climb the rope, surprising nearly
everyone by finally making it to the top.

As usual, however, Anastasia's triumph is short lived. Since there is
insufficient time in her English class to impress the foreign educators
with the poem she has memorized, Anastasia decides to recite it from
atop the rope and, gesturing to dramatize the poem, she lets go and falls
off. As a result, she ends up in the hospital where all of the novel's characters come together, helping her realize that she is "pretty special"
(*Answers,* 123). Ultimately, the act of rope climbing becomes a metaphor
for Anastasia's precarious journey toward adulthood, which she will
eventually achieve, although not without a few stumbles.

Three important interrelated subplots flesh out the rest of the novel:
Anastasia's relationship with her gym teacher, a black woman named
Wilhelmina Willoughby; the visit of Anastasia's Uncle George; and the
divorce of the Bellinghams, parents of her friend, Daphne. Despite her
disastrous date with Steve Harvey in *Anastasia on Her Own,* Anastasia is
still in love with the idea of romance. Her desire to climb to the top of
the rope, however, is closely connected to her realization that she has a
crush on her gym teacher, Ms. Willoughby. Convinced that she is weird
for having these feelings, Anastasia indirectly confides in her mother by
pretending that a friend of hers has this problem. Realizing that Anastasia is talking about herself, Katherine Krupnik reassures her daughter,
confessing that she once had a similar crush on her piano teacher and

that such feelings make her "normal, very sensitive, very capable of loving" (*Answers,* 52). By the end of the book, Anastasia is not ashamed of liking Ms. Willoughby, although she also fantasizes that her teacher might find romance with her Uncle George. This particular episode, Lowry has explained, grew out of an experience when, as a 10-year-old at summer camp in the Poconos, she developed a brief crush on a counselor named Jeanne.[3]

Anastasia's endeavors to matchmake for her uncle are another important part of the plot. At the beginning of the book, Anastasia's parents have traveled to California to attend the funeral of Anastasia's Aunt Rose. This is Anastasia's first brush with death since her grandmother passed away in *Anastasia Krupnik*. Anastasia is more emotionally distanced from this present death—she has not been close to her aunt. She is, however, grossed out by the cause of her aunt's death, salmonella poisoning (*Answers,* 6). Anastasia's brother, Sam, also has a hard time understanding the significance of his aunt's death and, much to Anastasia's embarrassment, insists on pretending his toy cars are a funeral procession. When her parents bring her newly widowed Uncle George back to Boston for a visit, Anastasia decides to help relieve his loneliness by finding him a new love-interest. After all, he looks just like Clark Gable. At first, she considers lining him up with Gertrude Stein, who politely turns down the offer. Then she arranges for him to meet Daphne Bellingham's recently separated mother.

Once again, Anastasia is briefly exposed to tragedy. Whereas Anastasia's parents seem secure in their love for one another, Daphne's are struggling, creating a new crisis for her friend. "Remember Alice in Wonderland," Daphne tells Anastasia, "how she drank from that weird magic bottle and ate that freaky cookie and went from large to small and back again? That's how I feel. . . . Family, no family. House, no house. Money, no money. Surprises every day. I never know when I wake up in the morning what that day's surprise will be" (*Answers,* 15). As with the death of her aunt, Anastasia initially does not know how to help her friend until, ever the romantic, she decides to find Daphne a stepfather.

Through these various subplots, Lowry explores the tension between fact and fiction, reality and romance, a common feature of the Anastasia series. On the one hand, Anastasia seems intent on discovering the complete facts about every situation she encounters. Learning to write news stories, she has been taught to ask, "Who, what, when, where, and why?" Each chapter except for the last ends with Anastasia's transforming some part of her life into a newspaper article.

Upon closer examination, however, these articles often reflect the young protagonist's daydreams instead of factual occurrences. In one article, Anastasia imagines that she makes it to the top of the rope, astounding her audience; in another, she sees herself straightening out Daphne about her parents' divorce. When the articles do report an actual event, Anastasia often overdramatizes the situation, as when she writes that she "plummeted" from the rope (*Answers,* 114).

Despite her desire to report the facts, Anastasia is still in love with the idea of romance. She wishes that she could read Margaret Mitchell's passionate *Gone with the Wind* in English class instead of Esther Forbes's *Johnny Tremain* (1943). When her father asserts that *Gone with the Wind* is terrible literature, Anastasia retorts, "But it's so romantic, Dad. I love romance. I wish someone would say to me, in a deep voice: 'Frankly, my dear, I don't give a damn.' Someone rich and handsome, with a mustache, like Clark Gable" (*Answers,* 8).

From the very beginning of the book, Anastasia is torn between her fascination with romance and the reality of the world. Hoping to be discovered by movie scouts, she wants to go to California to see the homes of celebrities. When she asks her mother to realistically assess her chances of this happening, Katherine Krupnik describes how mundane the trip will be, and Anastasia decides to stay home. Bothered that her aunt failed to die of something exotic, she is further disappointed when her attempt to bring her uncle and Daphne's mother together flops. Her chance to show off for the foreign educators in English class never materializes. Her one great triumph, finally climbing the rope, results in a trip to the hospital.

Yet Anastasia does make it to the top of the rope, and Ms. Willoughby does find Uncle George "charming" (*Answers,* 120). When Anastasia finally realizes that she herself is special, it seems clear that it is due in no small part to her romantic nature.

Of the later books in the series, *Anastasia Has the Answers* is one of the best. Anastasia's dilemmas are both more believable and poignant than her sudden dislike of her parents in *Anastasia, Ask Your Analyst* or her efforts to reform her mother's housekeeping in *Anastasia on Her Own*. A 1986 review in *The Bulletin of the Center for Children's Books* praises the novel, suggesting that, whereas some books in the Anastasia series "suffer from occasional desultory plotting and too-broad humor (although they are always entertaining), this one recaptures the freshness and heart of the earliest volumes, and Sam is rapidly assuming the position of the most off-the-wall scene-stealer since Ramona."[4] In 1989, *Anastasia Has the Answers* became the second Anastasia book to receive the Garden State Children's Book Award from the New Jersey Library Association.

Anastasia's Chosen Career (1987)

In *Anastasia's Chosen Career*, Anastasia again ponders her future, partly because of a school project, an essay entitled "My Chosen Career," which requires her to consider potential occupations. It is winter vacation of Anastasia's seventh-grade year and, after some persuasion, her parents allow her to take a modeling course in downtown Boston. This provides her with the opportunity to gain a broader view of the world, one not limited to her own suburban neighborhood. In the course of the novel, Anastasia is introduced to new aspects of her hometown, Boston. As she tells Henry ("Henrietta Peabody"), a black friend whose home in Dorchester she visits, she has lived in Boston all of her life and has never been to this part of town. Anastasia, of course, does not really believe she will become a model but decides that, as the advertisement for the course suggests, she could use a healthy dose of increased poise and self-confidence. At the same time, by going downtown she can interview a bookstore owner, a friend of her father, for her career project.

As in *Anastasia Again!* Anastasia's premature assumptions are shattered. Studio Charmante, the modeling school for teenagers, looks like it is part of a con game. The building that houses the school is a dump, and Anastasia and her friends quickly dub it "Cockroach City."[5] Anastasia decides to stick with the course, however, and comes away with exactly the renewed self-confidence that she anticipated. Like the studio, Barbara Page, owner of Page's Book Store, is also more than she appears to be. Although she has no real business sense, she is an enchanting conversationalist. What Anastasia eventually learns is that Barbara has a lot of people sense. Ultimately, Anastasia's adventures in Boston are successful. She gains a new friend, Henry; discovers a softer side to her old nemesis/friend, Robert Giannini, who has also enrolled in the modeling course; and makes tentative plans to work as Barbara Page's assistant in the future.

As in earlier books in the series, Anastasia is educated in the deceptive nature of outward appearances. As part of the modeling course, each of the students receives a makeover, which in some cases increases their confidence. Helen Margaret, a shy student whose hair is always in her face, emerges, in Anastasia's opinion, looking like actress Isabella Rossellini, while Henry Peabody, whose hair is clipped very short, becomes devastatingly beautiful. Even Anastasia looks prettier thanks to a new, shorter haircut.

Yet Anastasia soon realizes that, although her external appearance is important, she is still the same inside. She confides to her mother that she had begun to feel sorry for herself because, although her new haircut would make her look older, even prettier, she still is not going to be beautiful like Henry. Anastasia comes to the understanding, however, that Henry's beauty will be her ticket to a modeling career, something that she herself does not need because of the financial security of her own family. Anastasia's generosity toward Henry's potential success prompts her mother to comment that she is truly "a nice, nice person" (*Career*, 85). What Anastasia has gained is a new self-awareness, something that her pretentious fellow students, Robert Giannini or Bambie Browne, never obtain.

By the end of the book, Anastasia also gains insight into some of the people she meets, learning to look beyond their exteriors. Robert Giannini shows sensitivity when he comforts Helen Margaret Howell, who has good reason to be shy and nervous, having lost her parents and been badly burned in a fire. Henry Peabody becomes Anastasia's good friend and is much more caring than she initially appears. Like Anastasia, Barbara Page also turns out to be "a truly nice person," giving Henry a $35 book because it contains a photograph that looks like her.

The plot of *Anastasia's Chosen Career* is one that Alleen Pace Nilsen and Kenneth Donelson would describe as an "adventure-accomplishment romance," a work in which a protagonist overcomes self-doubts by accomplishing a quest.[6] Interspersed throughout the book are the multiple drafts of Anastasia's essay, which reveal her sometimes naive feelings about the world and her unrealistic view of what it means to pursue an occupation. Among other things, Anastasia writes that it is probably a good idea to take a modeling course to increase poise and self-confidence, that moving to another country may help one to avoid undesirable people from the past (such as Robert Giannini), and that a bookstore owner does not have to carry a gun. Her reports also detail her increasing admiration of Barbara Page, who has a heart of gold but not much business sense.

Concerned about the future, Anastasia gains some inner peace by reconciling herself to the fact that she is only 13 years old. She tells herself she has plenty of time to worry about the future. For now, it is "enough that she had a terrific week and had written a terrific paper" (*Career*, 141–42). Nevertheless, Anastasia cannot remain happy long. After making a mess of her essay's title when she types it, she gloomily tells herself that, instead of spending a week studying modeling, she should have taken a typing course.

As usual, reviewers noted the book's "mixture of wit and wisdom," its "funny adolescent dialogue," which is "true to their interests and language," as well as "the insight of an affectionate and perceptive observer of the human scene." This is a mixture, notes Dudley B. Carlson, "far too scarce in contemporary literature for adolescents, who respond to the thoughtful, reflective side of Anastasia as well as the flip side."[7]

All about Sam (1988)

With his growth spurt in *Anastasia Again!* Sam Krupnik has become one of the most popular members of the Krupnik family. Like Beverly Cleary's Ramona Quimby, who first appeared as a foil for her older sister, Beezus, and her neighbor, Henry Huggins, Sam began as a plot device, allowing Anastasia to experience sibling rivalry. Lowry's younger brother (the model for Elizabeth's baby brother in *Autumn Street*), her own children, and her grandson, Jamie, all undoubtedly contributed to the creation of Sam Krupnik.

Because of Sam's popularity as a character, Lowry received many requests for a book about him. At first, the idea seemed silly because Lowry and her editor believed that 3-year-olds would not be able to read about him and that 12- or 13-year-olds would not want to (Chaston 1994). Other children's writers, however, had successfully created books about characters younger than their reading audience. In Beverly Cleary's first Ramona books, for example, Ramona is much younger than most potential readers.

Ultimately, Lowry decided to try a book about Sam; the result, *All about Sam*, has appealed to a wide range of readers. Lowry explains, "The same kids who like Anastasia love those Sam books, but more than that it has extended the age range because kindergarten and first and second grade teachers love reading the Sam books aloud to kids. Kids that age relate to Sam, but also are enough older that they feel superior to silly old Sam." In addition, "each chapter is sort of complete in itself so a teacher reading aloud to children who are too young to read it can have a satisfying reading experience in one session and then the kids are eager for another, but they're not left incomplete. . . . Teachers in particular are eager for me to do another one" (Chaston 1994).

All about Sam recounts the life of Sam Krupnik from the time he is born through his family's move from Boston to Cambridge and through his "terrible twos." Although narrated in the third person, *All about Sam* takes the reader inside Sam's consciousness, beginning with his infancy. This idea is not unique. A television situation comedy, *Happy* (1960–61), and two later feature films, *Look Who's Talking* (1989) and *Look Who's Talking, Too* (1990), rely on the adultlike thoughts of infants for humor. In Lowry's book, there is often a disjunction between what the adults think Sam is feeling and his actual thoughts.

Because *All about Sam* covers more than two years of Sam's life, it includes some incidents that appear in the Anastasia series, although this time they are from Sam's point of view. As in *Anastasia Krupnik*, the newly born Sam waits eagerly for Anastasia to announce the name she has chosen for him. Sam also adjusts to moving, and he shoplifts a piece of Dentyne gum from the supermarket as in *Anastasia Again!* and *Anastasia on Her Own*. There are allusions to Sam's nemesis, Nicky Coletti, and Anastasia's science project involving gerbils, both detailed in *Anastasia, Ask Your Analyst*.

All about Sam itself is episodic; each chapter is a distinct incident in Sam's life that can be read independently: (1) Sam's birth, (2) his acquisition of verbal and large motor skills, (3) flushing Anastasia's goldfish, Frank, down the toilet, (4) toilet training, (5) moving to Cambridge, (6) beginning nursery school, (7) shoplifting a pack of gum, (8) acquiring a pet worm, (9) entering the public library's pet contest, (10) "show and tell" day at nursery school, (11) cutting his own hair, (12) trying to develop muscles, and (13) learning Morse Code.

Despite these disparate episodes, the book exhibits a thematic cohesiveness. Several of the chapters specifically deal with Sam's development of a personal identity. "Who *am* I?" he asks himself shortly after he is born.[8] A couple of pages later, he is pleased when Anastasia finally announces his name, and he comprehends that he is surrounded by his father, mother, and sister—his family. Later, when he cuts his own hair, Sam miserably announces, "I'm not Sam anymore." Instead, he has become "a porkypine. . . . An *ugly* one" (*Sam*, 109). Like many children, he has equated his identity with his appearance. In chapter 12, Sam asks his parents why he is called "Sam" and not "Son," wanting to know the difference between his name and his identity as a family member. In that same chapter, he also tries to change his concept of himself by building up his muscles. He is finally satisfied with his appearance, however, when he discovers that his father is not muscular either. In the last chapter, Sam learns Morse code so that he can send signals with his flashlight to his elderly neighbor, Gertrude Stein. The book ends as Sam flashes his name across the yard, prompting him to remember that he is "Sam."

Throughout the novel, Sam is also interested in finding his place in the outside world. He quickly advances through what psychologist Jean Piaget describes as the "sensorimotor period," in which he learns to control his body and is preoccupied with sensory experience, into the "pre-operational period," in which he acquires language and uses a very subjective logic. Frequently he frustrates other family members, who misunderstand his motives, yet he is clearly the object of their affection: Something about his childlike optimism and imagination endears him to others. This quality is illustrated when Sam adopts a pet worm and becomes a sort of parent himself. He is proud when his pet wins "First Prize . . . for Most Invisible Pet" (*Sam,* 89). He does not understand that every entry automatically receives a prize, nor that when his worm escapes, it is not the same worm that he finds outside his house. The pet contest depicted in this chapter is similar to one in which Lowry's own children entered their Newfoundland dog and, like every other child, won a prize. Sporting a paisley necktie, their dog "was designated 'Best Dressed Dog' " ("Newbery 1990," 421).

One could argue that the precociousness of the infant Sam is far-fetched. His frustrations with and appreciation of his world, however, are certainly credible, and the emotional content of the book rings true. Most of the reviewers of *All about Sam* predicted its appeal to younger readers. *Horn Book* maintained that "Childhood's problems and confusions have seldom been shown to a better, funnier, and more sympathetic advantage. Sam is a hero in the Ramona class."[9] *School Library Journal* forecast that "Sam and his loving family are sure to be a hit with anyone who has a younger sibling or has ever wanted one. The book also has sure-fire appeal to Anastasia's many fans, but it's too funny not to be shared with a class as a read aloud."[10]

A wildly popular book with young children, *All about Sam* has won more state children's book awards than any other of Lowry's books with the possible exception of *Number the Stars*. It has been honored with the 1990 Mark Twain Award (Missouri Association of School Librarians); the 1990–91 Charlie May Simon Children's Book Award (Arkansas Department of Education); the 1990–91 Mississippi Children's Book Award, the 1991 Prairie Pasque Children's Book Award (South Dakota Library Association); the 1991 West Virginia Children's Book Award, runner-up; and the 1992 California Young Reader Medal (California Reading Association).

Anastasia at This Address (1991)

Anastasia at This Address is Lowry's most fully realized look at an early young adult's notion of "romance," one that Anastasia eventually rejects for a more mature notion of love. Anastasia, whose first date in *Anastasia on Her Own* does not live up to her sentimental expectations, is ready to try again. Intrigued by the personals in the *New York Review of Books,* she decides to respond to "SWM [Single White Male], 28, boyish charm, inherited wealth, looking for tall young woman, non-smoker, to share Caribbean vacations, reruns of *Casablanca,* and romance."[11] After reading SWM's advertisement, Anastasia tells herself that they are both on the same wavelength. She, too, is tall and young, hates smoking, can recite all the lines in *Casablanca* from frequent viewing, would probably like a Caribbean vacation, and is "definitely ready for romance" (*Address,* 7).

Much of the book centers on Anastasia's correspondence with SWM. Telling stories through letters is a convention that has been popularized in such epistolary children's novels as Joan Blos's *A Gathering of Days: A New England Girl's Journal, 1830–32* (1979) and Beverly Cleary's *Dear Mr. Henshaw* (1983). Anastasia's nine letters to Septimus Smith (SWM) and his three replies are interspersed throughout the novel, each ending one of the 12 chapters and serving as humorous commentary on the action. To a careful reader, Anastasia's letters reveal that, although she is trying to be sophisticated, she is still young and innocent. In her first letter she explains that her education last year included learning how to write a friendly letter, which is why she is not using a formal heading. In her second letter she tells Septimus that she is "very interested in current events and things of international interest," such as "rumors of marital trouble between Charles and Diana" (*Address,* 20).

Anastasia's letters are full of quirky asides, all based on erroneous notions she has formed about Septimus. Since he is initially slow to respond to her letters, she assumes that he must be sick and advises him to drink lots of fluids and take aspirin. She questions his lack of response to her letters, which he must have received. After all, Peter Jennings's report about a postal truck colliding with live chickens did not mention that any mail was lost. Just in case the woman in California who wrote Septimus that she had a sloop happened to be movie star Debra Winger,

Anastasia announces in her seventh letter that *People* magazine says Winger has a young son. Luckily, before she can suggest that "he put his portfolio in with the garment bags on airplanes," she figures out what he means when he says that managing his portfolio takes up most of his time (*Address,* 92).

Septimus Smith apparently does not think that Anastasia's letters are odd. He, too, tries to read between the lines of the correspondence he receives and jumps to mistaken conclusions about their author. From her poor handwriting he assumes Anastasia is a doctor. Her pen name, "Swifty," suggests to him that she races the sloop she claims to own.

Unfortunately, Anastasia does not realize that Septimus is shallow and knows less about real romance than she does. Although he receives 416 letters as a result of his advertisement, he responds to only two of them, based on the photographs the writers send and the fact that they both claim to own a sloop. Because Anastasia sends him a picture of her mother, he does not realize she is a seventh-grader, despite the unintentional clues she provides him about her age.

At the end of the book, in a letter she never mails, Anastasia realizes how unrealistic the notion of a love relationship with Septimus is. "But the whole thing was really truly dumb on my part," she writes. "And the dumbest part is that I got to believing it myself a little bit" (*Address,* 116). Anastasia's childlike attitude toward romance has been dispelled. In this respect, she joins a large group of women in classic adult novels who are educated out of their unrealistic notions of love, characters such as Catherine Morland in Jane Austen's *Northanger Abbey* (1818) and Dorothea Brooke in George Eliot's *Middlemarch* (1871–72).

Part of Anastasia's education about romance comes from the novel's other main plot. Anastasia and her three best friends, Daphne Bellingham, Meredith Halberg, and Sonya Isaacson, all decide to give up the pursuit of boys since the ones they like do not reciprocate the time and attention they receive and are, ultimately, unromantic. (Anastasia reconciles this resolve with her pursuit of Septimus by rationalizing that he is a man and not a boy.) She even vows never to marry. She determines that her parents' marriage, for instance, is hindering their creativity and has clearly lost its magic: Her famous father is reduced to helping his three-year-old son dig a tunnel through his mashed potatoes instead of writing poetry, and her mother, an award-winning illustrator of children's books, is forced to create pot roasts instead of paintings. Anastasia momentarily decides she will become a feminist, which in her mind means imitating Daphne's divorced mother by giving up makeup.

Just when Anastasia and her friends have renounced boys, they are all asked to be junior bridesmaids at the wedding of Meredith's older sister, Kirsten. Despite their resolution, the girls are excited about the prospect of participating in a wedding. Contradictory as usual, Anastasia explains to her mother that she has given up boys, not weddings. Enthralled by the concept of romance, she wonders if she will ever become beautiful and how she will look in her bridesmaid's dress.

The wedding is successful but is clearly antiromantic. Anastasia panics because it turns out that Septimus Smith is also Meredith's "Uncle Tim," who is ushering at the wedding and who is clearly too mature for her. Furthermore, Uncle Tim mistakenly thinks Anastasia's mother is "Swifty" because Anastasia has sent him her photograph. The actual wedding ceremony is disrupted by fits of laughter: The bride and groom have received a large number of woks as wedding presents, and every time someone uses the word *walk* in the ceremony (including in the song "You'll Never Walk Alone"), many of those present laugh hysterically. Moreover, the four boys Anastasia and her friends have given up are all at the wedding and refuse to dance. The events of the novel do not leave Anastasia completely disillusioned with future romance. In the end, her mother explains that she does not regret getting married and that, if Anastasia truly renounces marriage, she may miss out on something valuable.

As in previous Anastasia books, wordplay is important. For instance, each of Anastasia's letters uses "SWIFTY" to create a different anagram describing herself, beginning with "Single White Intelligent Female: Tall Young" and finally ending with "Someday—When I'm Fourteen . . . ? Thank You" (*Address,* 8, 130). Furthermore, when Anastasia buys Sam's toy sloop, she can imply to Septimus that she has a real one, thus using language to deceive him without really lying.

Relying heavily on coincidence for its humor, *Anastasia at This Address* is carefully structured and less episodic than many later books in the series. How likely is it that the man Anastasia writes to would be related to her best friend? Actually, given Anastasia's character and penchant for attracting temporary mishaps, it seems quite believable. Reviewers have noted the humor of *Anastasia at This Address* and its strong interest for readers of earlier Anastasia books. Zena Sutherland suggests that "the appeal of this story will be in the comfort of a format that's expectable," while Diane Roback and Richard Donahue note that, although the "plot relies too heavily on coincidence, Anastasia herself is at her best here: headstrong, inventive, though not above learning from mistakes."[12]

Attaboy, Sam! (1992)

In 1992 Lowry focused on Sam Krupnik in *Attaboy, Sam!*, another book designed to appeal to younger readers. Unlike *All about Sam*, this book revolves around a single episode in Sam's life: his attempt to create a birthday present for his mother. As in the earlier book, Sam asserts his individuality, maintaining that he is all grown up. *Attaboy, Sam!* begins with Sam's learning to type his name, prompting a resolution to get rid of the magnetic letters on the refrigerator door since he does not "need baby stuff like those letters anymore."[13]

Almost immediately Sam concocts an idea to show how grown up he really is. His father and Anastasia have returned home depressed from Lord and Taylor's department store. They have just tried to buy Katherine Krupnik's favorite perfume for her upcoming 38th birthday. To their great disappointment, the perfume, Je Reviens, is no longer available. Katherine has said she wants no fancy gifts except for one bottle of this perfume. Secretly, Sam decides to collect his mother's favorite smells and create a new, special perfume just for her. "Attaboy, Sam," he tells himself with satisfaction at the prospect of pleasing his mother (*Attaboy*, 11).

The rest of the book involves Sam gathering various aromas that he keeps in an old jar. To create the perfume, Sam begins with a few drops of grape juice, adding some water and one of his father's pipes. When his mother announces that she loves the scent of babies, Sam accompanies Anastasia when she baby-sits young Alexander Parish, collecting "a scrunched-up poop-smelling tissue from the wastebasket by the changing table in the baby's room" and "a scrunched-up spitup-smelling tissue from the floor beside the rocking chair" (*Attaboy*, 33). Continuing to improvise, Sam adds a bit of chicken soup, vanilla extract, and some yeast because his mother says that fresh bread is the best smell in the world. Sam's pursuit of these odors, however, eventually gets him into trouble. He is accused of trying to cut the hair of everyone at nursery school when he clips a bit of his own hair to add to the concoction. Later, when his clothes get damp from the seawater he takes from the Boston Aquarium, his nursery school teacher thinks he has wet his pants.

In the end, however, Sam's well-intentioned present becomes a vile-smelling mess that explodes all over his room. He has suspected earlier that something is going wrong and becomes depressed at being unable to provide something nice for his mother. Ironically, both Anastasia and Myron Krupnik have made a mess of their homemade presents, too. Anastasia, who once wrote a fantastic poem in *Anastasia Krupnik*, writes one for her mother's birthday. The poem is worse than the one that Robert Giannini wrote in the earlier book because Anastasia now seems obligated to use rhyme. Myron Krupnik has enlarged a photograph of Katherine and painted over it. The result, Sam remarks, looks like one of the creatures in Maurice Sendak's *Where the Wild Things Are* (1963). Sam, Anastasia, and their father finally realize how funny the situation is. Myron Krupnik compares both Sam's perfume and Anastasia's poem to the smell that resulted when the garbage collectors went on strike in New York City. In the end, however, Sam saves the day. Earlier he has secretly taken in a kitten—named Purrfume—that now becomes Katherine's present.

Clearly the novel suggests that, although young children are likely to make mistakes, they can occasionally solve problems. More important, grownups are as capable of making mistakes themselves as are children. Lowry herself suggests that one of the nice things about this book is that, despite all of the disasters at the ending, "It's the little kid who saves the day and fixes everything and makes it all turn out okay and of course that's what little kids need to hear" (Chaston 1994). Lowry further explains that although the last chapter may be above the heads of little children, she loves the moment when "Dr. Krupnik has to show his terrible painting and Anastasia has to read her terrible poem" (Chaston 1994).

Once again Sam emerges as a likable, realistic child character. Like Anastasia, his life is full of contradictions: he wants to be an adult yet is clearly innocent and childlike. Hazel Rochman has noted the book's "hilarious denouement," arguing that Lowry "gently undermines the politically correct formula: "Sam's bored with dolls at nursery school—if they can't be named Rambo and exploded out of the doll carriages, he can't see any point to them—yet at the same time, he yearns to nurture a kitten."[14] Roger Sutton complains that the characters are "played a little lazily" and points out that "Sam, who knew Morse code at two, here gets kudos for tapping S*A*M on the typewriter."[15] Not surprisingly, *Attaboy, Sam!* has proven extremely popular with younger readers, as evidenced by its receiving the Garden State Book Award. *Attaboy, Sam!* was also one of *School Library Journal*'s Best Books of 1992.

Anastasia, Absolutely (1995)

Although Lowry had sworn she would never let Anastasia out of seventh grade, in *Anastasia, Absolutely* she finally begins eighth grade (Chaston 1994). Anastasia, however, is still unsure of herself and the world around her, as demonstrated by her responses to questions she is forced to write for a class in values, an idea that may have been inspired by the pamphlets *Personal Values* and *Values and the Family* that Lowry once produced. Anastasia's essays on values provide some of the best humor in the entire series.

The novel introduces a new character into the Krupnik family, Anastasia's dog, Sleuth, inspired by a Tibetan terrier named Bandit, whom Lowry acquired when she moved from Boston to Cambridge in 1993. In *Anastasia, Absolutely*, Anastasia faces an embarrassing moment when, on a morning walk with Sleuth, she must mail some sketches her mother has completed for a book. Instead of mailing the artwork, however, she inadvertently drops into the mailbox the blue plastic bag from her father's *New York Times*, which she has just used as a pooper-scooper. Convinced that her act constitutes tampering with the mail, Anastasia agonizes over what to do, especially when her friend Meredith tells her about four police officers who, that same day, descended on the corner of Chestnut and Winchester near the same mailbox, which has now disappeared.

Anastasia, who vacillates about her feelings in *Anastasia Krupnik*, still has a difficult time making up her mind. Should she call the post office and confess, especially since they will probably put her in jail? Anastasia's predicament is underscored by her "Values" class, in which the students debate and write about moral dilemmas. This time, instead of a mystery story or a report on a science project, each chapter of the novel concludes with Anastasia's response to an assignment about values. For example, would she kill a groundhog with a rock in order to save a vegetable garden that would feed a hungry family? (Probably, although she wonders whether the groundhog could be killed less painfully.) Would she sacrifice one day at the end of her life "in order to save the life of a small child in a Chinese village?"[16] (She probably would, although she would prefer that it be the day *after* her ninetieth birthday.) Unlike the responses penned by most of her friends, Anastasia seems to see two sides to every question. Although she assumes that her teacher, Mr. Francisco, will not like her "wishy-washy answers," he actually thinks she is "good at examining things, and seeing all the different options" (*Absolutely,* 82). After agonizing over what she should do, she confides to Mr. Francisco that she has inadvertently broken the law. He responds by telling her that "People always feel better if they do the right thing" (*Absolutely,* 84).

Anastasia's struggle to determine her own values is developed throughout the book. Trying to define her values, she starts to realize that maybe her friends do not think exactly the same way she does. In a related subplot, Anastasia's father becomes a jury foreman. In a parody of famous trials, such as the O. J. Simpson murder trial, which concluded the same year this book was published, Myron Krupnik discovers he is wishy-washy, too. Because the jury cannot decide what to do, Myron decides there must be "reasonable doubt" and announces a verdict of "not guilty" to the judge.

Anastasia's quandary over the mailbox mix-up is just one of her problems. She also has a crush on Mr. Francisco, who becomes one of the first nonrelatives to call her "pretty." Anastasia also has to assume responsibility for a new pet, something she has longed for, despite her ongoing relationship with her goldfish, Frank. (The kitten her mother receives from Sam in *Attaboy, Sam!* has been banished to the garage, but, luckily for her father's allergies, Sleuth is nonallergenic.) One of Anastasia's new responsibilities involves walking the dog, which allows her time to think.

In the end, Anastasia decides that she must admit that she has made a mistake in accidentally putting Sleuth's droppings into the mailbox. She returns home and calls the post office and, after Sam interrupts her, confesses that she tampered with the mail. Two police cars descend on the house, but it turns out that they merely want Anastasia's help in apprehending a man who has been putting bombs in mailboxes. One had been found in the mailbox near Anastasia's home but did not explode because someone had "dropped a bag of . . . dog doo-doo on it" (*Absolutely,* 102). In the end it turns out that the bomber was a surly man Anastasia noticed near the mailbox.

Anastasia's identification of the bomber is the culmination of several incidents in the novel, in which Lowry explores the uncomfortable side of fame, particularly the disjunction between public perceptions of celebrities and their real natures. This is a topic that likely has roots in Lowry's own growing notoriety that at times may seem daunting. Early in the novel, Anastasia reveals a time when a children's author visited her second-grade classroom to discuss a picture book about a zoo that she had written and illustrated. In a comic version of the kind of school visit Lowry has undoubtedly suffered through many times, the children are more interested in relating their experiences with zoo animals than in anything the writer has to say. Clearly, being a famous children's author does not immediately earn one either respect or adulation.

Similarly, by acting as models for characters in picture books that Katherine has illustrated, Anastasia's father and her dog both experience the uncomfortable side of fame. Whereas Anastasia enjoys finding a six-year-old version of herself in *Lucy Mousie*, her father does not appreciate being cast as the title character of *Uncle Dudley and the Dimwits*, especially in one picture where he is wearing "his underwear—striped boxers and a T-shirt" (*Absolutely*, 39). He moans that if anyone at Harvard ever saw his image in the book, "he would be ruined as a senior professor of English" (39). For Sleuth, becoming a character in a picture book also brings indignity since Anastasia's mother must use plastic barrettes to keep his hair out of his face.

As in earlier books in the series, Anastasia has developed a romanticized notion of fame through her exposure to popular culture. When her father serves as a jury foreman, she assumes that he has had fun, like the characters on the TV program *Night Court*. Not one minute of his experience, Myron Krupnik contends, has been fun. Even though various elements of the trial are like those that Anastasia has seen on television, the whole thing has been incredibly boring. "Don't you feel good, though, Dad?" Anastasia, still a romantic, asks him. "Because after all, if it weren't for you, an innocent man might have been convicted and sentenced to a life behind bars, and the real murderer would have gone free" (*Absolutely*, 66). Unfortunately, her father bursts Anastasia's bubble by explaining that the defendant was "an eighteen-year-old girl accused of driving without a license" (*Absolutely*, 66).

At the end of the novel, Anastasia is responsible for bringing a criminal to justice and finally becomes a legitimate celebrity. "Do you want to go public or not?" her mother asks her. "Be famous or not?" (*Absolutely*, 113) Anastasia, however, is not certain "that she wanted to be famous, under the circumstances" (*Absolutely*, 113). Like her trip up the rope in *Anastasia Has the Answers*, her success is not all that it is cracked up to be. In fact, it is embarrassing to be famous. Anastasia does not like having her picture taken by a newspaper reporter or the questions she is asked. She tries to follow the lead of her dog, who must pose with blue plastic barrettes in his hair so that a newspaper photographer can see his eyes. She imagines Sleuth drawing on the strength of noble forebears such as Rin Tin Tin and Lassie. In her mind, the dog muses, "I can sit here and look noble and pretend that I do not have this asinine and ridiculous hairdo" (*Absolutely,* 119). Anastasia follows suit, telling herself that she comes from a long line of truth-telling Krupniks, who do their homework, eat their vegetables, feed their goldfish, and act kindly to their younger brothers. "Therefore," Anastasia tells herself, "I am above embarrassment. I can stand here proud and tall, ignoring the fact that I am also a wishy-washy thirteen-year-old eighth grader who threw dog poop in a mailbox" (*Absolutely,* 119). Although her parents are legitimately famous (her father was once nominated for a National Book Award, and her mother illustrated a Caldecott Honor Book about elves), Anastasia does not take to the attention very well and must tell herself that, with her heritage, she is above humiliation, despite the fact that her biggest claim to fame has involved putting dog poop into a mailbox.

Once again Anastasia wowed many reviewers. *Kirkus Reviews* writes, "As usual Lowry . . . delivers tight, page-turning prose, plenty of humor, and characters right out of readers' neighborhoods."[17] A brief review in *Horn Book* finds Anastasia's new adventures "hilarious" and calls the book "light, satisfying reading."[18] Writing in the *New York Times,* Michael Cart, although extolling the virtues of the entire series, suggests that the plot of this book "is pretty pale when compared with earlier Anastasia adventures" but asserts that its strength, as with its predecessors, comes from its depiction of "a believably flourishing functional family" and "the author's subtle celebration of intelligence and the work of the creative mind."[19]

Anastasia, Absolutely exhibits many of the characteristics expected in a book about the Krupniks. The book is light, taking a potentially serious subject and finding humor in it and allowing the main character to demonstrate her considerable angst. As a character, Anastasia is every bit as charming as in the first book of the series and perhaps even a little more likable.

See You Around, Sam! (1996)

In Lowry's first book about the Krupniks, *Anastasia Krupnik,* Anastasia becomes so upset about the impending birth of her baby brother that she threatens to run away from home. In fact, she goes so far as to pack her most prized possessions—her paints, crayons, and an orangutan poster—in an old duffel bag that once belonged to her father. Anastasia's parents remain very calm during this episode, ultimately offering to let her name her brother in exchange for staying home. Lowry's most recent book about the Krupniks, *See You Around, Sam!*, focuses on a similar situation: This time young Sam decides to run away.

Comical tales about running away from home are the subject of a variety of children's books, many involving parents who humor their children, letting them discover for themselves the futility of their threats. Both Russell Hoban's *A Baby Sister for Francis* (1964) and Ezra Jack Keats's *Peter's Chair* (1967) feature children who briefly leave home until they are reassured that their parents care for them. In Beverly Cleary' s *Ramona and Her Mother* (1979), Ramona Quimby threatens to run away, only to be vanquished when her mother helps her pack her suitcase with more items than she can possibly carry. *See You Around, Sam!* uses similar situations but is both more developed and more humorous. In the tradition of folk and fairy tales, the novel features a circular journey, one in which the protagonist leaves home to face dangers and then returns to his family with increased status. In this case, however, the young hero's dangers involve a broken jar of peanut butter and a pair of plastic fangs.

Whereas *All About Sam* describes a couple of years in the life of Sam Krupnik and *Attaboy, Sam!* tackles a few days, *See You Around, Sam!* takes place during a single afternoon. As a result, it is the most focused of any of the Krupnik stories. Choosing a smaller lens than usual, Lowry effectively captures the limited world of a preschooler. Together with Sam, the reader travels down his street, meeting the ordinary but interesting people of his neighborhood. As in the earlier books in this series, Sam tries to establish his independence, yet ultimately reconciles himself to the fact that he needs the adults around him.

Like Anastasia, Sam decides to run away from home when he gets angry with his mother—in this case she has banned him from wearing the plastic fangs he got by trading his Etch-A-Sketch to his friend Adam. As with Ramona's mother, Mrs. Krupnik takes Sam's announcement rather matter-of-factly, telling him that the family will miss him, especially at dinner since they are having lasagna—one of his favorite foods. Sam leaves the house wearing his fangs, a fireman's badge, several Band-Aids, and a mustache created with eyebrow pencil. Armed with his father's gymbag containing a towel, his toy bear, and a pair of mittens, he determines to go to Alaska and live with the walruses. It is clear that Sam really only wants a little attention—he is disappointed when his mother says she will not cry when he leaves and merely asks for an address so she can write to him.

Sam's trip is actually quite short. As he leaves his house, Lowell Watson, the mail carrier, gives him the zip code for Sleepmute, Alaska, and safely escorts him to the home of next-door neighbor, Gertrude Stein. Next he visits Mrs. Sheehan and her young child, Kelly. Although Sam is not sure whether Kelly is a boy or a girl, he is pleased when he is invited to Kelly's birthday party until he remembers that he is running away. Since he has not said good-bye to his sister, Sam telephones her from the Sheehans'. As a result, Anastasia accompanies him to Mr. Fosburgh's house and then back to Gertrude Stein's to wake her up from her afternoon nap.

At each of his stops, Sam receives both advice and presents. On his first trip to Gertrude Stein's home, she offers him chocolate chip cookies and a snuggle on the couch, then reminds him that it is a long way to Sleepmute. Mrs. Sheehan provides him with an old baby blanket, two oranges, and a jar of peanut butter, along with the news that he will soon be eating a lot of fish and blubber. When Anastasia arrives on the scene, she comes bearing a leftover chicken leg and the story of how she too ran away, along with the advice that "It's considered very grown-up to change your mind after you've thought something over."[20] She also jokes that the bears in Alaska might want to eat a "Samwich." From Mr. Fosburg, Sam gets a flashlight and an atlas as well as a reminder that he will likely encounter "wildlife." Back at Gertrude Stein's, Sam receives a mink hat and the news that he will miss the November winding of her clock as well as the Thanksgiving festivities at his nursery school.

After each visit, Sam's neighbors send him on his way with the phrase, "See you around, Sam." This puzzling remark only adds to Sam's secret desire to return home. Pondering the meaning of "See you around," Sam realizes that by running away he is leaving his comfortable circle of family and friends. "See you around what?" Sam asks himself. The phrase sounds like his friends "were all in circle, like people playing Farmer in the Dell. People in a circle could see each other around." According to Mr. Fosburgh's atlas, Sleepmute is not a part of his circle: "Sam was heading in a long, straight line from Massachusetts to Alaska" and "*Nobody,* he realized, was going to see Sam Krupnik around" (*Around,* 71). At the same time, Sam becomes increasingly frustrated because no one seems terribly upset that he is running away.

Finally, getting hungrier and hungrier, Sam tries to loosen the lid of his jar of peanut butter by tapping it against the floor of Mrs. Stein's bathroom. When the jar breaks, Anastasia restores order, cleaning him up, putting a Band-Aid on his finger, and encouraging him to return home. Recognizing that he really wants to remain in the circle of his family and friends, Sam finally changes his mind about running away.

As in many of books about the Krupniks, *See You Around, Sam!* ends with a party—Mrs. Krupnik's lasagna dinner for the whole neighborhood. With everyone present whom he has encountered during his brief journey, Sam now tells them, "I just kept traveling all afternoon. I traveled in a big circle. And now I can see you around! . . . And you can see me around, too!" *(Around,* 100). Mrs. Krupnik provides everyone with gifts: glasses with fake noses for Steve Harvey and his father, a fake mustache for Lowell Watson, plastic cigars for Mr. Krupnik and Mr. Fosburgh, and red wax lips for Mrs. Krupnik, Mrs. Stein, Mrs. Sheehan, Mrs. Harvey, and Anastasia. Sam, too, receives a gift: another pair of plastic fangs. In an attempt at reconciliation, Sam's mother tells him she has changed her mind about fangs and asks for his forgiveness. However, chameleonlike Sam has also changed his mind. He asks if he can trade in the fangs for a pair of glasses with a fake nose.

See You Around, Sam! is filled with the same gentle humor as the previous Sam books. Although Sam's decision to run away seems to come out of the blue, his encounters with his neighbors are both believable and reassuring. All of the adults clearly care about him as they plot together to humor him. Sam's mother, too, is always present, making phone calls to her neighbors and watching him from the window of her house. Sam's safe return home and the communal celebration that follows is clearly in the tradition of the other Krupnik books. The search for a similar happy ending also propels the action of Lowry's more serious books, particularly *Rabble Starkey, Number the Stars,* and *The Giver.* As usual, Sam's adventures elicited praise from reviewers. Writing in the *Horn Book,* Roger Sutton argued that Lowry "invests an old story with truth, vigor, and laughs." He also writes that Lowry "respects both subject and audience, and while Sam is clearly prey to a host of adult good intentions, his cause is just and his dignity is ever intact"[21] (597).

It seems likely that the saga of the amazing Krupniks will continue. Few literary families have sustained so many books and experienced so many humorous mishaps. In *What's So Funny?: Wit and Humor in American Children's Literature* (1995), Michael Cart argues that "With wonderful wit, emotional honesty, and humor's saving grace, the Anastasia books artfully offer an education into understanding the world."[22] Although in recent years Lowry has gained literary acclaim for more serious works such as *Number the Stars* and *The Giver,* which are the focus of the next chapter, the creation of Anastasia and her family is itself an extraordinary accomplishment, one that will undoubtedly continue to attract young readers for years to come.

Chapter Five

Caroline and Company: In Search of Green Places

Despite the popularity of Anastasia and Sam Krupnik, Lowry has written a number of other humorous books in which she introduces new young characters who find themselves caught up in comic situations. Although these other characters are not quite as popular as Anastasia and although their stories are lighter in tone than works such as *A Summer to Die*, *Autumn Street*, *Rabble Starkey*, *Number the Stars*, and *The Giver*, they have all received critical praise. This acclaim demonstrates Lowry's ability to create exaggerated situations that are both hilarious and believable, while continuing to develop many of the important themes that have shaped her other work.

Like many of Lowry's books, the five novels and various short stories discussed in this chapter deal humorously with family life and childhood problems. The nature of the families in these books, however, differs from that of the Anastasia series. Unlike the Krupniks, the families in these books are either nontraditional or dysfunctional. Here the protagonists' parents are divorced (*The One Hundredth Thing about Caroline*, *Switcharound*, *Your Move, J. P.!*, and "Holding"), widowed ("Splendor"), or emotionally distant (*Taking Care of Terrific* and *Us and Uncle Fraud*), and the children often create new, extended families by finding role models in adults they meet outside their families. They also find new "homes" away from home—often "green places," as they are dubbed in *Taking Care of Terrific*: the New York Museum of Natural History, the Boston Public Garden, a temporarily vacant mansion, Central Park, and tree houses. Like Anastasia, the protagonists of these works are concerned with establishing their individuality, whether by taking new names, making unusual career choices, or falling in love.

The One Hundredth Thing about Caroline (1983)

The Tate family, the stars of *The One Hundredth Thing about Caroline*, *Switcharound*, and *Your Move, J. P.!*, were created in response to requests that Lowry write about a child whose parents are divorced. By this time, Lowry had presented her readers with a number of caring families (the Chalmerses, Armstrongs, Lorimers, and Krupniks), each with a father and mother who clearly love one another. The parents of the Tate children, however, have been divorced for some time. Their father, who has remarried and moved away, has very little to do with them, and their mother, who struggles financially, has the primary responsibility for their care.

Despite her different family background, Caroline Tate is to some extent a variation of Anastasia Krupnik. Like Anastasia, Caroline is smart, cultured, and lives in a big Eastern city, in this case New York. She is also opinionated and experiences sibling rivalry, although her brother, J. P. (James Priestly), is older than she is. Caroline's vision of the world, like Anastasia's, is occasionally warped by her premature judgments. Like Anastasia, who loves lists, Caroline enjoys compiling her activities on her calendar. For Caroline, an interest in paleontology takes the place of Anastasia's various efforts to become a writer. Like Anastasia, Caroline is a source of unending amusement and occasional exasperation to her mother.

In *The One Hundredth Thing about Caroline*, 11-year-old Caroline spends all of her time either roaming New York City's Museum of Natural History or helping her best friend, Stacy Baurichter, do "investigative reporting," which involves "investigative studies of their apartment buildings"—spying on their neighbors.[1] Unlike Stacy, whose father is a senior partner in a law firm, Caroline's family is not well-to-do. This means that Caroline and J. P. spend Saturdays doing housework and that their mother may serve them eggplant or parsnips for dinner because these items were on sale.

In Anastasia-fashion, Caroline quickly jumps to the conclusion that Frederick Fiske, "the Mystery Man who lived on the fifth floor," is a murderer because she finds a letter instructing him to "eliminate the kids" (*Caroline*, 13, 17). This discovery sends Caroline and Stacy off on a search for further information about Fiske. Stacy wrangles her way into the apartment building of Carl Broderick, author of the infamous letter, and learns from his mailbox that he is an "agent," which she assumes means he is a spy. When Caroline holds a new letter to Fiske up to the light, she discovers more instructions about "eliminating" the children. "I know it's tough, but you have to be brutal—and thorough—and quick," the letter says. This is followed by an admonition to find an obscure poison. Deciding that she needs help, Caroline consults her genius brother, J. P., who searches Fiske's apartment and turns up several clues: a *TV Guide* open to a listing for the mystery program, *Quincy*; a can of baby powder that might really contain arsenic; a pink rubber glove; and a dead mouse. For want of a better spot, the children hide this evidence in some rubber galoshes left behind by a man their mother had once dated. Later, when their mother, who is now dating Fiske, brings home some cannolis he has sent the children, they hide them in the galoshes, too, just in case they have been laced with poison.

While investigating Fiske, Caroline still finds time to visit the Museum of Natural History and talk to her friend and hero, Gregor Keretsky, "a vertebrate paleontologist, one of the world's experts on dinosaurs" (*Caroline*, 44). She has developed a theory that some people may have evolved from dinosaurs, including Frederick Fiske, whom she thinks resembles a Tyrannosaurus Rex. Although Keretsky does not take Caroline's dinosaur theory seriously, this does not prevent her from dreaming that she is pursued by a dinosaur with Frederick Fiske's face.[2]

The last three chapters of the novel detail a dinner party at which Caroline and J. P. plot to unmask Frederick Fiske as a potential murderer. J. P. wires Fiske's chair so that he will be stunned by an electric shock and the children can confront him about his murderous plot and call the police. The dinner party, however, does not go quite as planned. Fiske wears rubber-soled shoes, forcing Caroline to spill milk on his feet so that he will take them off. Then, when J. P. presses the button to activate the chair, he short-circuits the whole building, turning off all of the lights. Meanwhile, Stacy suddenly develops a crush on J. P., much to Caroline's chagrin, and announces that Fiske is too nice to be a murderer.

To pass the time while the lights are out, all of the characters reveal their dreams. Gregor Keretsky, it turns out, is yet another of Lowry's artist-figures. In a disclosure that anticipates the black-and-white world of *The Giver*, Keretsky explains that he gave up his career as a painter because he lost the ability to see colors. "The doctors could find no reason that my colors had disappeared," he tells the group (*Caroline*, 140). After this tragedy he went back to college to study paleontology. Although Joanna Tate always wanted to be a poet, she now works in a bank. This prompts Fiske to admit that, although he has a solid career as a professor of history at Columbia University, teaching "the same stuff year after year . . . was beginning to lose its color" (*Caroline*, 144). As a result, he has started writing a spy novel, which he sent to Carl Broderick, a literary agent. Broderick has told Fiske to eliminate the children in the novel because they are too flat. Now, however, courtesy of Caroline and J. P., Fiske thinks he can rewrite the book to breathe life into his child characters.

The lights come back on, both literally and figuratively, and Caroline realizes the mistake she has made. She is also stunned to discover that Fiske and her mother, as well as J. P. and Stacy, have been holding hands in the dark. The party disbands, and the novel ends with Joanna searching the closet for the galoshes so that Gregor can wear them home in the rain. When Caroline tries to stop her mother from finding the boots and discovering the hidden evidence, Joanna remarks, "The one hundredth thing I love about you, Caroline, . . . is that sometimes you're completely incomprehensible" (*Caroline*, 149). When Joanna locates the galoshes, the book concludes, "And the rest is too horrible to tell. Horrible horrible horrible" (*Caroline*, 150).

The One Hundredth Thing about Caroline, like the story Anastasia writes in *Anastasia Again!*, effectively parodies the conventions of adult mystery novels, poking fun at its heroine's misinterpretation of events and her preconceived notions. The amusing use of these conventions occurs in a number of children's books in which characters often make comical prejudgments. In "Being Detectives," chapter 2 of E. Nesbit's influential family story, *The Story of the Treasure Seekers* (1899), the Bastable children decide they would like to be detectives "and find out strange and hidden crimes." The children mistakenly jump to the conclusion that a gang of "coiners" or counterfeiters has infested the house next door. More recently, Ellen Raskin's *Figgs & Phantoms* (1974) and her Newbery-Award-winning *Westing Game* (1978) have borrowed stock elements from mystery novels to satirize their characters' prejudices. Although Caroline is wrong about her potential murderer, in the end it turns out that Frederick Fiske, Gregor Keretsky, Joanna Tate, and even the love-struck Stacy Baurichter all possess secrets and are not exactly what they seem to be. Like *Anastasia's Chosen Career*, the novel also explores the process of finding a profession. Even though Caroline, J. P., and Stacy all think they are sure of what they want to do with the rest of their lives, it turns out that most of the adults they know have been forced to alter their childhood dreams.

The One Hundredth Thing about Caroline introduces two very likable child characters who have prompted two sequels. The friendly rivalry between Caroline and J. P., as well as their particular family situation, sets them apart from Anastasia Krupnik, yet provides room for similar comical escapades. Most reviews of the book have concentrated on the novel's wit and structure. Zena Sutherland argues that the "book has less depth than most Lowry books, but it's just as clever, just as smoothly structured."[3] Both Ethel Heins in *Horn Book* and Kathleen Brachmann in *School Library Journal* note the strength of the novel's last scene. For Heins the reduction of the dinner party to a shambles "is like an old-fashioned slapstick movie."[4] Brachmann comments that Lowry keeps young readers in suspense until the dinner party, which "is both tense and humorous." She compares the book to those about Anastasia, explaining that, as usual, Lowry's style is "bright, fast-paced and funny, with skillfully drawn, believable characters."[5]

Taking Care of Terrific (1983)

Much of *Taking Care of Terrific*, one of the best of Lowry's humorous books, is set in the Boston Public Garden, a place Lowry knows well, since for many years she lived in an apartment on nearby Beacon Hill. The Public Garden becomes a sort of paradise where the characters can become whoever they want to be, at least temporarily. Although many of Lowry's novels have a distinct sense of place, this novel's setting is more concrete and specific than in some of the Anastasia books, which are set in the same city. With few exceptions, virtually all of the buildings and streets mentioned in the novel actually exist. Indeed, one could retrace the various trips that Enid makes to the Public Garden, to Joshua's apartment, and to Newbury Street merely by paying attention to the streets and intersections mentioned in the novel.

Taking Care of Terrific centers on 14-year-old Enid Crowley, a Bostonian girl with a lawyer father, who ignores her, and a hypercritical radiologist mother. The summer in which the novel takes place, Enid decides she wants more out of life than her great-aunt Enid, who did little more than "read all the novels of Henry James, one after another," and then begin them again, dying "with *The Portrait of a Lady* open in her hands at page 143."[6] Enid hates her name, which reminds her of the many words in Stephen King's horror novels that end with the letter *d,* such as "horrid, putrid, sordid, acrid, viscid, squalid" (*Terrific,* 5). As a result, she does what Anastasia Krupnik only dreams about: She adopts a name of her own choice, "Cynthia," which she uses when she meets new people. An aspiring artist, she has enrolled in classes at the Museum of Fine Arts and plans on spending all of her spare time in the Boston Public Garden, her "favorite green place," which is only two blocks away from her home. In the garden she decides she will find "romance, intrigue, danger, and pathos" (*Terrific*, 8). Enid is not far wrong. She takes a job baby-sitting Joshua Warwick Cameron IV, the four-year-old son of an over-protective socialite who gives Edith a list of rules that she proceeds to break as she takes Joshua to play in the Public Garden. Joshua, as it happens, is a kindred spirit and asks her to call him "Tom Terrific" instead of his real name.

Through various trips to the garden, the two children make friends with a bag lady who takes Tom Terrific to the bathroom in the nearby Ritz hotel and with a black saxophone player who calls himself Hawk. Neither of these new-found friends is actually what he or she seems. Hawk is really a sociology professor at Harvard, and the bag lady is Julia Simpson Forbes, widow of a millionaire, a woman "who lived all alone in a penthouse tower" at the Ritz and who "came down to wander each day in a Garden, where most people looked away when she passed because she was old" (*Terrific*, 162–63). With the help of Hawk and Seth Sandroff, the son of famous psychologist Wilma Sandroff, Enid actually does find "romance, intrigue, danger, and pathos." When Julia Simpson Forbes, whom the children know simply as "the lady in the black coat," complains that the park no longer has root beer Popsicles, which remind her of the root beer her father used to make, Enid decides to stage a protest. "What if all you had in the whole world, besides a black bag and a chilly doorway, was a memory of a father who once made root beer, and sometimes a Popsicle that brought that memory back?" Enid asks. "And what if they took that little bit of comfort away without asking you?" (*Terrific*, 45). With the help of 18 additional "female derelicts," Enid and her friends picket the Popsicle cart in the Public Garden, convincing the vendor to reinstate root beer Popsicles (*Terrific*, 85).

One evening, Enid, Seth, and Tom Terrific are in the park when the famous swan boats are being chained up, and Enid wishes that she could take all of the bag ladies for a ride at a time no one else would bother them. Enid and Seth soon concoct a plan to hijack one of the boats and take the bag ladies on an evening ride. Enid and her friends successfully carry out their scheme, riding the swan boat on the pond, accompanied by Hawk playing "Stardust" on his saxophone and with the whole group singing along. As the trip ends, they discover the police waiting for them, and the group is arrested. Eventually all of the charges against Enid are dropped, but she is forbidden ever to see Tom Terrific again.

The novel concludes with an epilogue, which Enid's housekeeper, Mrs. Kolodny, tells her frequently appears in books with "sad endings" to make clear that "the sad ending was only temporary" (*Terrific*, 165). This wrap-up reveals that the events in the Public Garden have changed Enid and that she has affected the lives of others as well. Enid and Seth, whom she once described as having the personality of a rattlesnake, are now good friends. That Seth is able to tell Enid and Tom Terrific that he loves them, just before the police take him away, suggests how much he has changed. At the end of the novel, Tom Terrific secretly calls up Enid and tells her he now has a governess, another kindred spirit who calls herself "Wonder Woman." Tom Terrific's vitality apparently has not been broken by his repressive mother as Enid had feared. After Enid and Tom announce that they love one another, Enid doodles her name on the phone pad, this time turning it into "SPLENDID" (*Terrific*, 168).

Taking Care of Terrific shares several themes with the early Anastasia books. Like Anastasia, many of the characters in the novel judge others by their initial appearances. It does not occur to Enid that Hawk might be a university professor, that her bag lady might be a millionaire, or that Seth might have a heart. At the same time, Enid, like Anastasia, does not like her name but comes to appreciate it in the end. As in *Anastasia Krupnik*, memory is also an important factor in the plot: Enid's plan to protest the loss of root beer Popsicles is waged in part to help the bag lady retain the memories of her father.

The importance of maintaining romance in one's life is also one of Lowry's favorite topics. Like the children in *Us and Uncle Fraud*, which was published the following year, Enid values places and people that provide magic in her life. Early in the novel, she discusses *Moby-Dick* with Mrs. Kolodny. According to Enid, Mrs. Kolodny probably imagined that going whaling involved "harpooning whales, and then sipping a piña colada and taking a swim at St. Croix." She also probably thought Gregory Peck (the star of the film adaptation) would come along. Enid concludes that the "problem with most people's lives is that they have lost the capacity to believe that Gregory Peck would be along" (*Terrific*, 13). For a moment, Enid, Seth, Tom Terrific, Hawk, and their bag lady all have the ability to believe that Gregory Peck just might be along. In your "green place," Enid tells Tom Terrific, you can be any age you want to be and you "could be Tom Terrific" (*Terrific*, 26).

The spiritual transformation of young children through green places is a familiar theme in children's novels. In Lowry's own preface to an edition of Francis Hodgson Burnett's *The Secret Garden*, she writes that the "image of a garden as an inviolate place, a place for withdrawals, renewals, and beginnings, is one that spans the history of literature."[7]

Lowry mentions that she herself created such a place in *Taking Care of Terrific*, quoting Enid, who says that "everyone needs a green place in his life, a place where you can be whatever you want to be, a place where you feel alive and ageless" (*Terrific*, 25). Like Mary and Colin in *The Secret Garden*, Enid and her friends blossom in their green place. To some extent, Lowry manages to capture what she praises in Burnett's novel, the "satisfaction of feeling all the inhabitants of the secret garden—rose-bushes, fruit trees, and children—emerge with tantalizing slowness into new growth, and finally into lush bloom" ("Garden," xiv).

An early critique in *Kirkus Reviews* suggests that Lowry did not intend for the book to be viewed as realistic. It also argues that "the fantasy comes off as a silly, sentimental-liberal pipe dream that trivializes the realities she wants to transcend."[8] Other reviewers have also noted that the plot initially seems unlikely but argue that Lowry makes it believable and satisfying. Zena Sutherland writes that the various elements in the plot come together in a story that is "touching, inventive, believable, and hilarious."[9] Karen Jameyson also notes that the "Boston setting is vividly evoked. . . . The strength lies . . . in the author's ability to create a strong heroine whose determination and humorous outlook override her confusion and difficulties."[10]

Taking Care of Terrific was made into a short film that aired on the *Wonderworks* television series in 1987. Some of the weaknesses of this film, which Lowry does not care for, point out the original novel's strengths. Most important, the novel is removed from its Boston setting and placed in a rather generic park, which lacks the reality of Lowry's descriptions. At the same time, Enid and the other children are not very well developed. Lowry herself notes that she finds it absurd that, in the film, Enid's father says he will not be home for dinner because he is going to argue a case before the Supreme Court. "Surely he would have mentioned that before," Lowry says. "It would be the pinnacle of any lawyer's career" (Chaston 1994).

Us and Uncle Fraud (1984)

The year after Lowry published *The One Hundredth Thing about Caroline* and *Taking Care of Terrific*, she produced a somewhat more serious work, once again creating a new protagonist, Louise Cunningham. Much of *Us and Uncle Fraud* focuses on Louise's relationship with her eccentric Uncle Claude. *Us and Uncle Fraud* is narrated by 11-year-old Louise (a variation of Lowry's own first name) Cunningham, whose nickname, "Lulu," is the same as Lowry's favorite childhood comic-book character. Louise lives in a small, unnamed town built on "the eastern bank of a sluggish, tan river with an Indian name."[11] Although the novel is intentionally vague about the town's geographic location, Lowry writes that "the town had certain things in common with Carlisle, Pennsylvania, where I spent my childhood. For example, the local college's biology building, rumored to contain dead babies in jars . . . a vivid memory from my own early years. My town had no river though" ("Letter").

Louise's 14-year-old brother, Tom, seems to be turning into their father, emulating his political opinions. He also wants to go into the newspaper business like their father, who edits the local paper. Louise spends more time with her younger sister, Stephanie, who is 2 ½, and her 10-year-old brother, Marcus, who leaves notes for her in a hole in the wall between their bedrooms.

On Good Friday, their mother's brother, Claude, descends on the Cunninghams for one of his infrequent visits; the last took place three years before. Louise's father is less than thrilled by Claude's arrival and suggests they do not have room for Claude to stay, while Tom refers to their uncle as "Claude the Fraud" (*Fraud*, 4). Louise's mother, however, defends her brother, asserting that he is "a very considerate boy" although he is 35 years old. "Isn't that odd, that I always think of Claude as a boy?" she chuckles (*Fraud*, 7). At first Uncle Claude is a disappointment to Louise: There is nothing special to distinguish his face, and Louise decides that he looks like a turtle.

Nevertheless, Louise and Marcus soon succumb to their uncle's charm. At the mention of Louise's name, he begins to recite a risqué limerick and regales them with anecdotes such as the history of handshaking. Most riveting of all, he confides to them that a small box in his possession contains "secrets" and "surprises" for "certain children" (*Fraud*, 12). Eventually Claude tells Louise and Marcus that the box holds very special Easter eggs that he has supposedly smuggled out of Russia—hollow eggs encrusted with jewels that contain "a whole tiny world" inside (*Fraud*, 47). Claude will not show the children the eggs; they must be hidden, and Louise and Marcus will have to search for them. On Easter morning Claude is nowhere to be found. He has left behind a letter, urging the children to search hard for well-hidden treasures, followed by the unintelligible words, "*Ya tebya lyublyu*" (*Fraud*, 56).

During Claude's brief visit, Louise and Marcus take him on a tour of the town. When Claude asks them to show him "the most interesting, exciting, dangerous, *secret* thing" in town, they take him to the Leboff house, a miniature version of a Norman castle. The children's friend Kenny Stratton, the son of the Leboff's driver, has shown them where the key is hidden, and the children like to sneak inside during the Leboff's annual visit to Europe. The same day that Claude mysteriously departs, it is revealed that the Leboff house was robbed. Louise and Marcus begin to wonder whether their uncle might have committed the crime.

The town is soon inundated with rain that precipitates a flood. On the way home from school, Marcus makes a detour to the cemetery to look for bones that might be floating out of the graves. In what Laura Zaidman describes as "the most exciting drama in any of Lowry's books," Louise goes back to look for Marcus, as does Tom who is swallowed up by the flood (Zaidman, 258). This scene recalls the ending of a famous nineteenth-century British novel, George Eliot's *The Mill on the Floss* (1860), in which Maggie Tulliver and her estranged brother— another authoritarian boy named Tom—are swept away in a flood as they try to help the townspeople. Unlike Tom Tulliver, the Cunningham children are all safe, although Tom lapses into a coma.

While Tom lies unconsciousness, Louise has time to think about her uncle and finally recognizes that he has lied to the children since they have never found the eggs he is supposed to have hidden. At length Louise asks her mother why she does not hate Claude. "You've known him his whole life, and he probably lied to you all the time," Louise says (*Fraud,* 127). Her mother responds that Claude is different and that, although he drinks too much and cannot hold a job, he tries "hard, still, to create worlds for himself, worlds where he is rich and where he can give wonderful gifts" (*Fraud,* 126). His imagination, her mother tells Louise, is a gift in itself.

As Tom remains unconscious, Louise and Marcus tell him their secrets and find themselves repeating to him the strange words from Claude's letter: "*Ya tebya lyublyu, ya tebya lyublyu*" (*Fraud,* 130). One of the nurses overhears the children and recognizes the words, which, it turns out, are Russian for "I love you." Shortly after this discovery, Tom wakes up. The events of the past few months have affected Louise and her family. Tom has not really changed, but she and Marcus have altered in their knowledge of things. "We loved Tom, and we had not truly known that before," Louise explains, adding that she now realized that Claude had really lied but accepted it "because he was part of our family, and because he loved us" (*Fraud,* 147). Happily, it turns out that Claude did not rob the Leboff house; the crime was actually committed by

Kenny Stratton's father, a fact that Louise inadvertently discovers during the flood when she picks up a stolen pitcher he had been holding.

One of the novel's major themes is symbolized by Claude's nonexistent Russian eggs. The real eggs, Claude has explained, contain miniature magical worlds and scenes that are visible from a hole in one end. Throughout his life, Claude has merely tried to create similarly imaginative worlds. Louise's mother relates that, as a child, Claude turned a tree house into a magical world for the neighbor children, one replete with its own special rules, language, and religion. For Claude, "it really was a whole world; it seemed quite real to him, and important, and he forgot that it was all just a pretend thing" (*Fraud,* 82). In the end, Claude manages to communicate some of his special perspective to Louise and Marcus. As Marcus explains, the fact that their house might have a treasure inside makes it look different. Now it was special because Claude had visited there and because it contained a treasure. At the end of the book, Louise recognizes in her home "the regular sounds of family life and of the love that bound us together, despite our flaws." That recognition, she explains, "was Claude's real gift" (*Fraud,* 148).

In some ways, *Us and Uncle Fraud* is the book that, in tone and theme, most closely resembles *Autumn Street*. Both books are bittersweet and involve a brush with death that changes their narrators' views of the world. The town of *Us and Uncle Fraud*, which is never named, might well be the same one described in *Autumn Street*. Moreover, although the book does not establish a particular time period, a few details—such as references to grainy black-and-white spy motion pictures and Technicolor extravaganzas, visits to the movies every Saturday afternoon, and listening to the radio (with no mention of television)—suggest that, like *Autumn Street*, it is set in the past. Elizabeth Lorimer and Louise Cunningham's movement from innocence to experience also seems similar.

Critics have commented that *Us and Uncle Fraud*, although exhibiting characteristics of many of Lowry's books, is somewhat different in tone from most of her comic works. Ethel R. Twichell believes that the book "exudes a warm family feeling, although it does not have the acerbic humor or smart-alec zest of the Anastasia books."[12] Zena Sutherland writes that the book has "Lowry's usual wit, humor, and polish" as well as "more drama than some of her other books."[13] Lynn Littlefield Hoopes notes the overall seriousness of the novel's theme, explaining that although "the story's meaning surfaces a bit suddenly at the end, the idea of family unity and what can be accomplished through love is compellingly brought forth."[14]

Switcharound (1985)

In *Switcharound*, which was published the same year as *Anastasia on Her Own*, Lowry returns to characters introduced in *The One Hundredth Thing about Caroline*. Casting about for a plot, she remembered that Caroline and J. P. had a father who had not appeared in the first book and decided to send them to Des Moines to visit him. Lowry jokes that this is a "fraudulent book, set in a place I've never set foot." Unlike the previous book about the Tates, Lowry opted not to do firsthand research by visiting Iowa. Instead she created a "generic neighborhood" that she called Des Moines. The kids who really live in that region, she explains, "think it's terrific that there's a book in Iowa" (Chaston 1994).

In *Switcharound*, Caroline and J. P. have been sentenced to spending the summer in Des Moines, Iowa, with their father, his second wife, their six-year-old son, "Poochie," and their infant twin daughters, Holly and Ivy. Neither J. P. nor Caroline is happy about the situation. Caroline will now miss the special week devoted to primates at the Museum of Natural History, and J. P.'s plan to spend the summer building a computer will certainly be complicated. Neither Caroline nor J. P. feels especially close to their father, who calls them "princess" and "fella," never writes to them, and has his secretary merely renew magazine subscriptions for their Christmas and birthday presents. Furthermore, Caroline, like Anastasia Krupnik, is prejudiced against suburban life and cannot stand the thought of spending the summer in Des Moines. "You can't trust a city that doesn't pronounce its final consonants," Caroline mutters.[15] She also worries about what children wear in Iowa and whether she will make any friends there.

When Caroline and J. P. arrive in Des Moines, things are even worse than they expected. Caroline is saddled with caring for the twins while her stepmother, Lillian, goes to school to get her real estate license. Meanwhile, the very unathletic J. P. is forced to coach Poochie's baseball team. Both Caroline and J. P. decide to take revenge on their father and his new family: J. P. determines he will sabotage the baseball team by using the weaknesses of individual team members, and Caroline resolves to switch the twin girls around. Since Holly always wears pink and Ivy dresses in yellow, this is a relatively simple task. After they are bathed, Caroline allows the girls to play naked in a playpen so that even she is not sure which one is which. Eventually Caroline and J. P. regret their plans for revenge. Caroline realizes that she really likes the twins even though she does not enjoy caring for them. She and J. P. also begin to feel sorry for their father when it turns out that he may be going bank-rupt. Worst of all, one of the twins develops an earache and is going to be treated with penicillin, which will cause an allergic reaction if the twin is really Holly.

By the end of the novel, however, everything is neatly resolved. J. P. saves his father's sporting goods store by revealing that his financial woes are due to a computer error. Caroline takes over J. P.'s coaching duties and leads the "Tater Chips" to victory, partly due to a bunt by Poochie, which turns into a home run. As Caroline writes her mother in the last chapter, "Now that everything is switched around, J. P. and I actually like Des Moines quite a bit" (*Switcharound,* 118).

The theme of the novel is embodied in the title, "Switcharound," which symbolizes Caroline and J. P.'s whole summer. To begin with, their entire way of life has been switched around because their father has the right to demand that they stay with him for the entire summer, an option he has never before exercised. Initially Caroline feels that life is very different in Des Moines. "Where were the museums?" she asks her-self (*Switcharound,* 22). Can she stand to stay in a house that looks like something out of "Leave It to Beaver," "My Three Sons," "Father Knows Best," and "The Donna Reed Show"? (*Switcharound,* 24). By the end of the story, however, Caroline's feelings have flip-flopped. She discovers that there are museums in Des Moines, but, more important, she also learns to care about her father and his family.

To some extent, Caroline's transformation comes about when various members of the family are switched around as well. J. P. is a disaster as a baseball coach, a role his father has imposed on him. When J. P. demon-strates his strengths by using his computer knowledge to save the day, his father learns to appreciate him. Caroline, who does not fare well as a baby-sitter, is actually quite good as a coach and, when she assumes that role, leads the team to victory. Poochie, who desperately wants to suc-ceed in baseball, is failing because he has poor eyesight and is batting right-handed. When he switches the way he bats, he too becomes more successful. In the end, the novel suggests that individuals should be allowed to develop their individual talents. No one, as it happens, is really identical. Even the twins, Holly and Ivy, are different; Caroline discovers that one has a mole and the hair on their heads grows in differ-ent directions.

Switcharound, like the other books about the Tates, is light, humorous fare. Like much comedy, however, it relies on coincidence. For example, it seems highly unlikely that the moment the twins are switched, one will need a penicillin shot and might be allergic to it. The exaggeration of the situations, however, is part of the book's charm. Despite Caroline's disdain for situation comedies of the fifties and sixties, the humor in *Switcharound* draws from the tradition of programs like "Leave It to Beaver" and "Donna Reed." What is different, however, is the freshness of Caroline and J. P., who refuse to become stereotypes like their father and his second wife.

Switcharound has proved popular with both adults and children. A review in *Bulletin of the Center for Children's Books* argues that, although the last chapter too conveniently ties up loose ends, "the strong characterization, the humorous style and yeasty dialogue, and the change and development (including some shaking of stereotypical sex roles) in the two main characters give the story both substance and appeal."[16] Both Laura Zaidman and Kristiana Gregory also praise Lowry's characterization of Caroline and J. P. "The strong relationship between brother and sister is exceptionally well portrayed," writes Zaidman, "demonstrating the same fun and mutual affection (observable between arguments) seen in their earlier banding together to get revenge against Frederick Fiske" (Zaidman, 259). Gregory adds that "Young readers are bound to identify with these injustices of childhood and also the warmth within a caring family."[17] *Switcharound* has attracted young readers across the United States. In 1988 it received the Prairie Pasque Award from the South Dakota Library Association and in 1989, the Maryland Children's Book Award from the Maryland International Reading Association.

Your Move, J. P.! (1990)

Like Anastasia Krupnik, whose younger sibling went on to star in stories of his own, Caroline Tate's brother, J. P., became the protagonist of one of Lowry's novels, *Your Move, J. P.!* The action of the book apparently takes place before *The One Hundredth Thing about Caroline* because J. P. is 12 and Caroline is 10. Like *Anastasia at This Address*, which Lowry would publish the following year, *Your Move, J. P.!* explores the humorous complications of young love, although this time Lowry presents them from a male point of view. Fans of Lowry's other books had been demanding a story about a boy, and J. P., who had already stolen scenes in *The One Hundredth Thing about Caroline* and *Switcharound*, seemed a likely candidate.

During the past few years, teenage romances featuring young boys have become increasingly popular. Like *Your Move, J. P.!*, these books are generally humorous, poking fun at their protagonists' infatuations. A good example is Jerry Spinelli's *Space Station Seventh Grade* (1982), in which another seventh-grade boy finds himself acting crazy to attract the attention of a female classmate, only to discover that he may like someone else. Several critiques of Lowry's book have suggested its connections with other stories in this genre. Ilene Cooper compares the novel to an episode of the television program *The Wonder Years* (1988–93), which, she argues, "it resembles in both voice and plot" because it "is awash in emotion yet able to make fun of itself at the same time."[18] Ruth Ann Smith suggests that J. P. is a cousin to Betsy Byars's Bingo Brown, the protagonist of novels like *The Burning Questions of Bingo Brown* (1988) and *Bingo Brown and the Language of Love* (1989).[19]

As the novel begins, J. P. Tate suddenly has the desire to use deodorant for the first time in his life because Angela Patricia Galsworthy, a girl from London, has enrolled in the Burke-Thaxter School, where he attends the seventh grade. "It had never occurred to him . . . that this might someday happen," we are told. "Now it had. James Priestly Tate was in love."[20] J. P.'s infatuation with Angela, he soon learns, prompts this otherwise sane and scientific boy to do things he would usually consider crazy. To begin with, he starts telling lies in hopes of attracting Angela's attention. When Mrs. Hunt, their teacher, asks if anyone has a map of London so that Angela can show the class where she lives, J. P. raises his hand, prompting a frantic search for a map, which is resolved only when Caroline brings him one from a travel agency. J. P. soon concocts a story that Raymond Albert Myerson, a former student who had died, was actually his cousin. Like his "cousin," J. P. is supposed to have a rare disease, "triple framosis," which makes Angela feel sorry for him. J. P.'s obsession with Angela also takes his attention away from chess, one of his favorite hobbies, because he is practicing dancing and figuring out how he will kiss Angela when the time comes.

J. P. hopes the kiss might take place when he escorts Angela to the Spring Fling dance, part of the school's annual celebration of the arrival of spring. The students are supposed to come to school in costume, and a number of other activities are planned, including J. P.'s championship chess match against Kevin Kerrigan. Like the dinner party in *The One Hundredth Thing about Caroline* and the wedding in *Anastasia at This Address*, the protagonist's plans for a perfect day begin to backfire. J. P. has come up with the idea that he and Angela should go to school dressed as golf bags since their costumes are supposed to relate to spring. J. P. does not realize that their costumes will prevent them from sitting down all day, including during his chess match, or that it will be nearly impossible to go to the bathroom. During the day, J. P. hopes to avoid Angela's father, who she says is a world-famous physician specializing in nervous disorders, and Raymond Myerson's parents, who are visiting the school. Unfortunately, J. P. cannot prevent Angela from hearing the Myersons tell how their son died in a boating accident (not from a fatal disease).

Unsure of what to do, J. P. leaves the school after winning his first chess match to consult with Ralph, a man who spends his days in Central Park and who claims to have a disease for every letter of the alphabet. Ralph, who has previously advised J. P. about his "character flaws," suggests that he stop lying and tell Angela the truth. In the course of their discussion, J. P. realizes that he has been lying to himself as well and that he is not in love with Angela. As in *Taking Care of Terrific*, an apparently homeless person from a large city park helps the protagonist to gain insight into himself.

The trip to the park makes J. P. late for his second-round chess match. Meanwhile, J. P.'s friend Hope disguises herself with his golf-bag costume, taking his place in the second round of the chess match, which she loses. J. P. consoles Hope by explaining that, if she had won, it would have been cheating—another lie. In the end it turns out that Angela has also been lying: Her father is not a doctor. Ultimately J. P. begins to appreciate Hope's friendship and, when he takes her to meet Ralph, starts creating an alphabet of his positive character attributes, including honesty and integrity. For the first time in months, J. P. feels "weightless, and completely unencumbered" (*Move*, 122).

Although *Your Move, J. P.!* ends with a fairly specific message about the importance of honesty, it steers clear of outright didacticism, largely through its humorous tone. From the outset, J. P.'s romance is comical and is never treated very seriously. Nor is the novel's climax a surprise. Lowry invites her readers to laugh at J. P.'s universal dilemma and to root for his inevitable breakup with Angela.

Once again, Lowry uses a literary allusion to reinforce her themes. Here it is Mark Twain's *Prince and the Pauper* (1882), a book that J. P.'s class is reading. Had J. P. read Twain's novel more closely, he might have noted similarities to his own situation. Like the protagonists of *The Prince and the Pauper*, J. P. pretends to be different from what he really is and in the end discovers it is better to be himself. As in Twain's novel, Lowry's story even includes a scene in which someone else (Hope) literally takes the protagonist's place. As Edith Twichell has suggested, *Your*

Move, J. P.! is an entertaining sequel to the other Tate books and "makes a good case for the dangers of mixing lies and love."[21] Other reviewers have noted Lowry's "keen sense of the absurd" and "sympathetic understanding of early adolescent angst" (Smith, 169).

Short Stories

In the past few years, Lowry has occasionally returned to writing short stories, the genre that first brought her to the attention of Houghton Mifflin. The stories she has written vary both in sophistication and intended audience but explore many of Lowry's major themes, including the need for magic, tolerance, and diversity in the world. "Splendor," which appeared in *Short Takes: A Short Story Collection for Young Readers* (1986), is a gentle story in which a girl and her mother discover they both have a similar desire for magic in their lives. Thirteen-year-old Becky falls in love with a red dress in the window of a store called "Chrysalis." For Becky, the dress, which has hundreds of gold-sequined stars on the skirt, represents "beauty; music; happiness; grace and glory and glittering change"—in other words, "Splendor."[22] With a little encouragement from her mother, Becky decides to buy the dress with her baby-sitting money so that she can wear it to the school Christmas dance. When her older sister, Angela (another annoyingly perfect older sister like Molly Chalmers in *A Summer to Die*), tells Becky the dress is "trashy," Becky has second thoughts. She continues to have doubts about the dress, which is too big, and she is afraid that everyone will laugh at her. She does not have to go to the dance, however, because she comes down with a fever.

Later, however, she feels better, and her mother shares a special memory with her. Her mother had bought a rather hideous purple dress nine years ago when Becky's father had died. At the time Becky's mother had thought she had wanted the dress more than anything else, and when she wore it occasionally in private, it made her feel like "something magic would happen" ("Splendor," 102). The mother and daughter put on their dresses and dance together. "It'll be our secret," Becky's mother tells her, "that we had our own party, and that upstairs in the backs of our closets, we have hidden away—" Becky finishes the sentence with "Splendor" ("Splendor, 104–5). For Becky and her mother, like Louise, who needs her uncle's secret in *Us and Uncle Fraud*, and Enid and Tom Terrific with their secret identities and magical park, it is important to have a secret—something that makes life special and magical.

In 1990, Lowry contributed "The Harringtons' Daughter" to *A Gathering of Flowers* (edited by Joyce Carol Thomas), an anthology of stories representing childhood in America from the point of view of writers from a variety of cultural backgrounds. "The Harringtons' Daughter" focuses on a brief moment in the life of its 17-year-old narrator, Nina. While Nina's mother is ill, she comes to stay with her grandparents, whose next-door neighbors, the Harringtons, have a daughter who reputedly is crazy. Nina meets the Harringtons' daughter, Sigrid, whom she mistakenly thinks is named "Secret." Nina eventually learns that Sigrid's son had died in a boating accident. Later Nina encounters Sigrid again, this time on her own side of the fence, and gives her some hollyhocks. When Sigrid becomes upset because she wanted to be all alone, Nina responds that she is "losing someone, too," but that she does not want to be all alone.[23] Nina leaves the summer behind and stays home from college to share time with her mother. The Harringtons' daughter, however, kills herself. Nina concludes that in "years to come, I would encounter other secrets and would grow to understand the wish to draw the shades against them. Sometimes the memory of the Harringtons' daughter kept me from doing so" ("Daughter," 33–34).

The voice and tone of "The Harringtons' Daughter" is similar to that of both "The Recital" and *Autumn Street*, and Sigrid Harrington's behavior is reminiscent of Mrs. Bigelow's in *Rabble Starkey*. The bittersweet quality of the memories in this story allow Lowry again to explore one of her favorite themes: confronting the real problems and dangers of the world. Although Elizabeth Lorimer and her father tell each other that bad things will never happen again, they are only pretending. Indeed, the inability to experience tragedy is one of the most destructive qualities found in the world that Lowry creates in *The Giver*. Even though there is little plot to "The Harringtons' Daughter," its concern with human suffering looks forward to *The Giver*.

Lowry has also contributed to two thematic collections of stories and poems by well-known children's authors and illustrators. The first of these, *The Big Book of Peace* (1990), collects stories and pictures that explore the idea of peace by such familiar names as Lloyd Alexander, Natalie Babbitt, Jean Fritz, Katherine Paterson, Jerry Pinkney, and Maurice Sendak. Lowry's contribution, "The Tree House," focuses on two neighbor girls, Chrissy and Leah, each with a tree house and a sign that says, "KEEP OUT!"[24] Chrissy begins a feud between the girls when she refuses to let Leah visit her tree house because "It's just for me" ("Tree House," 31). This prompts Leah to tell Chrissy she hates her, to which Chrissy responds, "I hate you, too" ("Tree House," 32). For several weeks the two girls refuse to talk to one another until the day Chrissy offers to lend Leah some books, and Leah gives her a banana. The two girls lend each other various items, rebuilding their friendship, and eventually use a board to create a bridge between the two tree houses. At the end of the story Leah asks Chrissy, "What do you think is the best part of a tree house?" and her friend replies that the *very* best part is the bridge" ("Tree House," 37–38). Like Enid Crowley of *Taking Care of Terrific*, Chrissy and Leah find their own special green places, which are more meaningful when they are shared. As in many of Lowry's novels, great happiness occurs when two children bridge their differences and become friends.

The Big Book for Our Planet (1993), published three years after *The Big Book for Peace*, is a similar anthology devoted to environmental concerns. Lowry's contribution, "Elliot's House," is a somewhat cryptic, cautionary tale about the way garbage seems to be taking over the world. Ms. McKreutzer has asked the students in her class to draw pictures of their homes, which they change whenever their houses are altered. One boy, Elliot, draws a rather ordinary house. During the weeks that follow, however, he adds bags of garbage. When Ms. McKreutzer asks Elliot if the garbage is going to be picked up, he matter-of-factly states that his family throws it out the window because "We like to do it that way."[25] Little by little, Elliot adds new details to his drawing, including more mounds of garbage that cover his windows, an old, broken-down refrigerator, some dead fish, tires, and cars without tires. This continues until one day Elliot does not come back to school.

The other children miss him, wondering what other details he would have added to his picture. A couple of children try to brighten Elliot's picture with zinnias and poodles, but they notice that his house is already covered up with the garbage he has drawn. When the whole class takes the school bus to Elliot's address to look for him, all they find is a messy vacant lot in which steam shovels and caterpillar tractors are scooping dirt around and a sign that says, "Landfill." When the children return to school, they miss Elliot, but after a while he is only "a dim memory," and when his picture becomes faded it is thrown away and recycled ("Elliot's," 121). Whether Elliot has literally been covered up with garbage or merely moved somewhere else is not quite clear; certainly waste has, for all intents and purposes, taken him away from his classmates.

In 1994 Lowry's "Holding" appeared in another thematic anthology, *Am I Blue?*, a collection of short stories for young adults on gay and lesbian themes. The protagonist of the story, a boy named Willie, travels to New York to visit his divorced father, whose friend, Chris, has died. During Willie's visit, he attends Chris's funeral and helps comfort his own grieving father. When he returns home, Willie finally tells his best friend, Jon, that Chris, his father's "significant other," was "a guy."[26] He also reveals his own grief over Chris's loss, prompting Jon to comfort him briefly, before Willie playfully tells his friend that he smells as if he overdosed on Right Guard. In the introduction to the collection, Marion Dane Bauer suggests that Lowry's story "touches not just on the world of a gay father, but on the tender awkwardness of two teenage boys in a 'male bonding' session."[27]

None of the works in this chapter has received as much critical attention as Lowry's Anastasia books or the award-winners discussed in the next chapter. Nevertheless, they are well-crafted studies of children grappling with many of Lowry's favorite themes. *Taking Care of Terrific* and *Us and Uncle Fraud* treat some of the same issues as Lowry's earlier work but seem more consciously directed toward a young audience. Although the Tate books never confront the serious themes of *Anastasia Krupnik*, they are truly funny and present protagonists who will undoubtedly endear themselves to young readers. Many of these works, including Lowry's short stories, deal with friendship and diversity, reflecting some of the concerns of Lowry's most widely acclaimed novels, the focus of chapter 6.

Chapter Six

What Friends Do: *Rabble Starkey, Number the Stars,* and *The Giver*

In an almost unprecedented editorial in the July/August 1993 issue of *Horn Book*, Anita Silvey praises *The Giver*, suggesting that reading the book "resembles the experience of suddenly seeing an amazingly composed oil landscape created by someone you had passionately admired for their black-and-white character sketches." According to Silvey, Lowry risked a great deal in producing a novel unlike her usual "contemporary novels," which typically feature engaging characters and explore functional families.[1] In the eighties and nineties, Lowry has continued to take risks that have resulted in her three most widely acclaimed novels: *Rabble Starkey, Number the Stars*, and *The Giver*. On the surface, these three books may seem very different. The first is a realistic, contemporary novel about the daughter of a young single mother living in Virginia; the second is a historical novel set in Denmark during World War II; and the last takes place in an imaginary dystopian world of the future. All three books are more serious than those about the Krupniks and Tates, and, with the exception of *Autumn Street*, they are richer than Lowry's earliest novels. Deceptively simple, yet poetic and emotional, these novels represent Lowry at her best. Despite their superficial differences, however, they are all closely related in both plot and theme. Each is concerned with the concept of family, which Lowry once said was the topic of all of her books ("Visit"). They also explore a philosophy espoused in *Number the Stars,* the belief that friends help each other because "That's what friends do."[2] Each of the three books is a quest story involving both a physical and a psychological journey on the part of the main character, ending with its protagonists in a state of transition, without a definite resolution. Like all of the novels discussed so far, they are also concerned with the power of literature and personal memory. In fact, *The Giver* can be read as the culmination of all the ideas about memory in Lowry's other books, from Meg Chalmers's photographic remembrance of her sister and Natalie Armstrong's broken green panther through Elizabeth Lorimer's memory painting and Anastasia and Sam's "inward eye." In addition, *Rabble Starkey, Number the Stars,* and *The Giver* appear to be the books most likely to stand the test of time, ensuring Lowry's critical reputation in the future.

Rabble Starkey (1987)

When *Rabble Starkey* was first published in 1987, Ann A. Flowers commented that its protagonist is a winner, "a surprising and invigorating change from her usual, but always admirable, suburban, middle-class protagonists."[3] In an eloquent essay published in a critical anthology, *The Voice of the Narrator in Children's Literature,* Lowry writes that the book began with the voice of a "surprising and invigorating" protagonist, Rabble Starkey. Lowry explains that she began to formulate the novel with two sentences that came unbidden into her head: "We had a big war in our neighborhood that summer, and the only one on my side was Gunther. And shoot, Gunther was worthless as sin, he was only five and he had pinworms to boot."[4] Lowry wrote those sentences down and, after mulling over them for a long time, began to fashion a story out of them. By the time she had completed the novel, those sentences had disappeared, but they provided her with a voice that was very different from Anastasia Krupnik's and Elizabeth Lorimer's, whose lives, like Lowry's, are "secure, almost predicable; conventional, comfortable, and safe" ("Voice," 182). Like *Number the Stars* and *The Giver, Rabble Starkey* is different from many of Lowry's books. In it Lowry wanted to write about "families of an unconventional sort, whose lives were to be less predictable, less secure" ("Voice," 182). "I think given the fact in our culture families are now taking different forms," Lowry explains, "that has to be addressed in books." *Rabble Starkey* is about "people caught in their particular circumstances" who "are nonetheless a family—and they create a particular family which is not like the family I grew up in or what we used to think of as a family" (Chaston 1994). Eventually, Lowry also discovered the novel's setting, the foothills of the Appalachian mountains, where Lowry's brother, Jon, lives and works as a doctor. Lowry listened to the voices of that region and used them to help create Rabble and her mother.

Rabble Starkey is one of Lowry's favorite novels. In a personal interview, she reveals that she became very fond of the characters, in particular, Rabble's mother. Although Lowry was conscious that she was writing a fictional story, Rabble's mother—Sweet Hosanna (called Sweet-Ho) —seemed to change and move her life along on her own. Lowry also enjoyed showing how a piece of literature can open up a child's world, as *The Red Pony* does for Rabble. "It was great fun," Lowry says, "to have that child's use of language improve gradually as her life changed" (Chaston 1994).

Rabble Starkey centers on a 12-year-old girl, Parable Ann ("Rabble") Starkey, and her mother, who had run off to get married at the age of 13, returning home shortly thereafter without her husband. Rabble has spent the first eight years of her life with her grandmother, "Gnomie," and the last four with her mother and the family she works for, the Bigelows. Both the Starkeys and the Bigelows are concerned with creating a stable family life despite difficult problems. At the beginning of the story, Rabble recognizes that she and her mother are "just hired help at the Bigelows," that they do not own a house, and that the neighborhood does not really belong to them, a fact that her archenemy, Norman Cox, frequently taunts her with.[5] When her sixth-grade teacher, Mrs. Hindler, gives her class the assignment of making family trees out of construction paper, Rabble bemoans the fact that she does not even have any brothers and sisters although she does have a number of cousins. As she tells her mother, "I don't have no brothers or sisters at all, just my one dumb apple sitting there all alone in the middle. I wish I could've been twins. . . . Or that you got married again, maybe, and—" (*Rabble*, 14). Rabble's best friend, Veronica Bigelow, has a brother, a father, and a mother as well as a "bedroom all ruffled up and fancy" in a real house (*Rabble*, 7). Veronica, however, feels abandoned by one of her parents, her mother, who has been mentally ill since the birth of Veronica's younger brother, Gunther. According to Rabble, Veronica's mother "wouldn't be called normal." She "don't talk" and "don't do much" except "empty things" like going "around the house smoothing the beds all the time" (*Rabble*, 31).

As the novel progresses, Rabble, Sweet-Ho, Veronica, Gunther, and Mr. Bigelow seem to be merging into one big happy family. When Veronica's mother is hospitalized, this time for nearly drowning Gunther by "baptizing" him in a creek, Rabble and Sweet-Ho move into the Bigelows' guest room to help take care of the family. Rabble already feels like Gunther is her brother because "he stayed at our place so long when he was little, and Sweet-Ho is motherly to him, and all" (*Rabble*, 29). The longer Rabble and her mother are with the Bigelows, the more it seems as if they are really one family. When Rabble, Sweet-Ho, and Gunther go on an outing while Veronica is visiting her mother at the hospital, Rabble allows a waitress to believe that Gunther is her real brother, referring to the absent Veronica as her sister and Mr. Bigelow as her father.

Both Rabble and Veronica develop a sincere, sisterly closeness. They both dress as gypsies for Hallowe'en and humor Veronica's younger brother. They lend each other the names of family members for their family-tree project and share their feelings as they discover that boys in their classroom have crushes on them. When Norman Cox throws a stone at the elderly Millie Bellows on Hallowe'en night, they spend time helping the woman and adopt her into their family. Because Rabble cares for Veronica, she decides not to embarrass Norman Cox (now Veronica's boyfriend) by revealing that he was the one who injured Millie Bellows. Rabble and Veronica even develop a fantasy that they will grow up and live together in the old Rockwell house (a possible allusion to the popular American painter Norman Rockwell, who idealized family life in his covers for the *Saturday Evening Post*), providing a home for orphans and hiring the ladies who write verses for Hallmark cards to help care for them. "So it was just us, just our family, at Christmas," Rabble remarks, speaking of their holiday celebration (*Rabble,* 160).

Mr. Bigelow, too, seems to have adopted Rabble and Sweet-Ho. He buys them sweaters, an act that gives Rabble "a strong feeling of belonging" (*Rabble,* 73). Later he pays for Rabble's party dress for her first boy-girl party. He also reads to the children and encourages Sweet-Ho to consider going back to college. On Christmas night, Rabble even discovers Mr. Bigelow and Sweet-Ho kissing. Mr. Bigelow's parents also seem to have accepted Rabble and Sweet-Ho. When they are ready to leave from their Thanksgiving visit, Grandpa Bigelow gives Rabble a crisp new five-dollar bill, and Grandma Bigelow says she should be proud of her mother, right before kissing them both on the cheek.

Notwithstanding Rabble's desire for a traditional family, the fantasy family life that the Starkeys and Bigelows have created cannot last forever. Mrs. Bigelow begins to get well and soon will be coming home. The idea that Rabble's relationship with the Bigelows will now change frightens her. "I can't go back and live in a garage again, Veronica," she tells her friend. "I just can't. Not after being a family altogether. Not after us being like sisters all this time" (*Rabble,* 176). Rabble soon discovers that she will not have a say in what happens. Sweet-Ho has decided to attend college in Clarksburg and leave the Bigelow's employ. She tells Rabble that she and Mr. Bigelow have been pretending to have a different kind of love for each other from the one they really feel. As she and her mother drive off toward their new destination, Rabble half expects to see her long-lost father on the curb. "But there was nothing there," she writes. "There was only Sweet Hosanna and me, and outside the whole world, quiet in the early morning, green and strewn with brand new blossoms, like the ones on my very best dress" (*Rabble,* 192). In an article in the *Writer,* Lowry discusses the ending of three of her novels, *Anastasia on Her Own, Find a Stranger, Say Goodbye,* and *Rabble Starkey,* explaining that they all feature main characters moving forward in some way.[6] Certainly Rabble and her mother are moving ahead to a new life. Not surprisingly, Lowry notes, the British edition of *Rabble Starkey* is titled *The Road Ahead.*

During the course of the novel, Rabble is slowly educated about the real meaning of the words *home* and *family.* Early in the story, Rabble has to write an essay called "My Home," much of which focuses on the objects in her house, although she ends by suggesting that feelings are the most important thing in the home. For another school assignment, Rabble has to replace some of the words in her essay using a thesaurus, and the result is both humorous and artificial. When it comes time to leave the Bigelows, Rabble again revises the composition: "All of these things together give my home the good feelings that it has. No matter where a home might be, feelings are the vital thing" (*Rabble,* 188).

Throughout the book, Rabble comes to realize that there are many different kinds of families. When her teacher puts up the various family trees that her class has created, Rabble notices that they are not all the same, revealing to her that other people have problems, too. For example, Parker Condon's grandmother has been married twice, and Diane Briggs's sister has died. Through her interactions with Millie Bellows, Rabble becomes acquainted with yet another kind of family, a single elderly woman whose only son died years before when he was 14. One of Rabble's classmates, Norman Cox, the son of a Presbyterian minister, comes from a seemingly traditional family. Indeed, he makes fun of Rabble because she lives in a garage. Yet Norman, obsessed with drawing pictures of bombs, is the one who injures Millie Bellows and is always in trouble with the police.

Eventually Rabble also learns that individuals must continue with their lives despite tragedies. After Veronica's mother is hospitalized, Rabble ponders the fact that things go on much the same, even after enormous changes have taken place. What happened to Dorothy, Rabble asks herself, after she returned home from Oz? She "just went back to school, same as always, and took spelling tests and played kickball at recess, I expect," although she probably had nightmares now and then

(*Rabble,* 57). Similarly, when Millie Bellows dies, Sweet-Ho cries but, that same night, goes to her class and earns the second-highest grade on the exam she takes. Later, when Veronica's mother is returning home, Sweet-Ho refuses to let that fact deter her from her goal of gaining an education. Sometimes, Rabble realizes, people can do no more than to say "Sorry for your trouble" and bring casseroles, as Mrs. Cox and Millie Bellows do when Mrs. Bigelow is hospitalized (*Rabble,* 54).

As in many of Lowry's books, a subtheme of *Rabble Starkey* is the value of literature. Despite the fact that she uses improper grammar, Rabble is interested in language and words. Her mother, too, enjoys books and ultimately decides to study literature. More importantly, two of Lowry's own favorite books, John Steinbeck's *The Red Pony* and Marjorie Kinnan Rawlings's *The Yearling*, help Rabble understand her own situation. Mr. Bigelow reads aloud *The Red Pony* to Rabble, Veronica, Gunther, and Sweet-Ho, bringing them all closer together. The girls in particular are enraptured by the book. Describing the feelings it produces, Rabble explains, "I could scarcely breathe, waiting for what came next" (*Rabble,* 133). For Christmas Mr. Bigelow gives Rabble a book about yet another boy named Jody, *The Yearling*. At the very end of the book, Rabble tells her mother that both *The Red Pony* and *The Yearling* are about the same thing, "all kinds of loving, and about saying goodbye. And moving on to where more things are in store" (*Rabble,* 191).

Although Rabble's voice is different from that of Elizabeth Lorimer's, *Rabble Starkey* is the closest in tone to *Autumn Street* of any of Lowry's other books. Both books are about a strong, albeit temporary, friendship between two children as well as their interactions with relatives and friends. Like *Autumn Street*'s Elizabeth and Charles and *Number the Stars'* Annemarie and Ellen, Rabble and Veronica forge a close relationship despite apparent differences in their family backgrounds. All of these books suggest that even when friends are separated, their relationships can last.

Based on a July 24, 1986, letter from Lowry to her editor, the manuscript of *Rabble Starkey* underwent a thorough revision after it was originally submitted for publication.[7] According to Lowry, she softened the character of Norman Cox, fleshed out the role of Parker Condon, and clarified the relationship between Sweet-Ho and Mr. Bigelow. Lowry did not, however, change the name of Rabble's mother, which, one of the readers had noted, means *whore* in Black English vernacular. Her response was that most of her readers would not be aware of this possible meaning.

Early reviewers of *Rabble Starkey* recognized the book as different from some of Lowry's other family stories and praised the character of Rabble. In a review in the *New York Times*, Lou Ann Walker writes that "Rabble has a fine and delicate sensibility, particularly when facing the impossible choices."[8] Betsy Hearne contends that, in the end, the novel portrays "a large, diverse cast by focusing the point of view as one of a maturing observer."[9] On the other hand, Kathleen Brachmann in *School Library Journal* criticizes the book as "almost soporific," arguing that readers learn more about characters other than Rabble, despite the fact that she is the narrator. "Lowry's fans will read this despite its flaws," she concludes, "but it's a disappointing effort."[10] Most readers do not agree with Brachmann's assessment. Indeed, in 1987 *Rabble Starkey* received three important awards: the *Boston Globe-Horn Book Award* for fiction, the Golden Kite Award for fiction from the Society of Children's Book Writers, and the Child Study Award from the Children's Book Committee of Bank Street College.

Number the Stars (1989)

As already mentioned in chapter 1, *Number the Stars* was inspired by stories that Lowry's good friend Annelise Platt told her about growing up in Denmark during World War II. Details of Platt's story, such as the Nazis' black boots and wearing mittens to bed soon inspired a story about a young girl who helped the Danes smuggle the Jewish population out of the country in 1943. By the end of the week that she and Platt spent together in Bermuda in 1988, Lowry was convinced she could tell this story.

Despite the setting of *Autumn Street*, Lowry, who writes mostly contemporary fiction, found herself doing historical research at the Atheneum in Boston. There she came across a photograph of Kim Malthe-Brunn, who was shot for his participation in the Danish resistance movement. Discussing the novel's development, Lowry writes, "I had the facts—they were all there, in the books in The Atheneum basement. And I had the characters and plot—they were all there, in my imagination at first, and by now on the pages I'd written and rewritten. I had the details Annelise had provided" ("Journey," 100). At that point Lowry felt that she needed to visit Denmark. She had been there before but could no longer "feel" the country. On a four-day trip Lowry visited the sites mentioned in her book. She stood on the coast north of Copenhagen, looking across at Sweden, as Annemarie and Ellen do in the novel, and on the balcony of an apartment, imagining the celebration in the street below that took place when the war ended in 1945. In Copenhagen Lowry met Kristin Krough, who would have been a young bride during the occupation and who, along with her husband, had been involved in the Danish resistance movement. It was Krough who told her that Annemarie's mother might well have read and loved the American novel, *Gone with the Wind*. Lowry's trip to Denmark also provided another important detail that appeared in the novel, a pair of shoes made of fish skin.

After completing her original manuscript, Lowry did additional revisions for accuracy, including eliminating a reference to apple pie, changing the day of the week for the Jewish New Year in 1943, and substituting the "Kattegat" for some references to the "Baltic Sea." She also attempted to soften the Nazis somewhat in one scene and altered her description of Ellen Rosen to keep her from becoming a stereotype.[11] According to Lowry, at one point her editor asked her to excise from the manuscript some of the references to the boots. Lowry did not, however, make the change, arguing that from the vantage point of a frightened child who could not see the soldiers' faces, the large boots would be terrifying ("Newbery 1990," 420).

Ultimately, all of Lowry's research and revision paid off. It would garner for Lowry her first Newbery Medal, as well as a number of other awards, including the Sydney Taylor Book Award from the Association of Jewish Libraries; state awards for children's literature from Illinois, New York, and Arkansas; and *Parenting*'s Reading Magic Award. Although the novel does not try to explore all of the horrors of World War II, it constitutes an accessible introduction to the subject, one that provides readers with hope while also suggesting some of the tragedies associated with the Holocaust. It is at once a suspenseful tale about a young heroine who plays a role in saving her best friend and her family and who faces great danger on several occasions. The story is peppered with allusions to folktales such as "Little Red Riding Hood" and novels like *Gone with the Wind*. The novel also explores important themes for young readers, including the nature of true friendship and bravery.

Number the Stars focuses on the friendship between 10-year-old Annemarie Johansen, a tall, blond, Lutheran girl living in Copenhagen, and her neighbor, Ellen Rosen, who is short, dark-haired, and Jewish. Even though Lowry goes to great lengths to suggest that on the surface the two girls are very different, they thoroughly enjoy each other's company, whether they are running races or playacting with paper dolls in

Annemarie's apartment. Both of the girls are clearly imaginative: Ellen enjoys acting in the school play, and Annemarie tells stories to her younger, sometimes irritating, sister, Kirsti.

In the very first chapter, however, it becomes clear that the German occupation of Denmark will threaten the two girls' friendship. Annemarie, Ellen, and Kirsti are racing down Østerbrogade Street on their way home from school when they are stopped by Nazi soldiers. Although nothing much comes of this encounter, Annemarie's mother tells the children that they must guard their behavior, pretending to be nothing but faces in the crowd. For the children, the Nazis have become a fact of life, and it is difficult to remember a time when food was not scarce and curfews were not in effect. For Kirsti, the war merely means that children ride bicycles with wooden wheels, wear shoes made out of fish scales, and forgo pink-frosted cupcakes. The adults, however, understand the dangers and grief that the war has already brought: Annemarie's older sister, Lise, has been killed by Nazis for her part in the Danish resistance, a fact that Annemarie will not learn until the end of the war. Nevertheless, a few things have not changed: Annemarie still attends school and likes to spend time with her best friend.

Early in October of 1943, however, things begin to get worse. Jews in Annemarie's neighborhood, like the button shop owner, Mrs. Hirsch, and her son are being taken away by Nazis, and it appears that Ellen and her family are also in danger. Like Annemarie and Ellen, the Johansens and Rosens are close friends. Thus, when the Rosens are threatened by the Nazis, the Johansens help them simply because, as Mrs. Johansen remarks, "That's what friends do" (*Number,* 24). The novel explores the great lengths to which the Johansens, particularly Annemarie, go to prove their friendship, one that will continue despite the fact that the Rosens are forced to flee to Sweden.

Because it would attract too much attention for the Rosens to begin their journey into exile together, the Johansens agree to take Ellen in, pretending that she is their own daughter until she can be transported to safety. On the evening of the Jewish New Year, Ellen comes to stay with the Johansens. In one of the most suspenseful scenes in the novel, Nazi soldiers descend on the Johansen apartment in the middle of the night, searching for the Rosens. Annemarie's father tells the soldiers that Ellen is one of their daughters and, when questioned about Ellen's dark hair, produces a photograph of his dead daughter, who, as an infant, was dark. Just before the Nazis arrive, Annemarie notices Ellen's

Star of David necklace; terrified for her friend, she pulls the ornament from her friend's neck and conceals it in her own hand.

In the second half of the novel, Annemarie, her mother, and her sister take Ellen to meet her parents at Annemarie's Uncle Henrik's farm, which is near the coast. The Johansens and the Rosens are about to become a part of an important historical event: the transport of over seven thousand Danish Jews to Sweden during a 48-hour period of time. Since the beginning of the war, life in the country has not changed as drastically as it has in the city, although Henrik complains that the Nazis have "relocated," or taken, his butter. From the shore near Henrik's house, Annemarie can see the coast of Sweden, where Ellen and her parents must go to obtain safety.

The trip to Uncle Henrik's is fraught with danger—the Nazis are everywhere. They question Annemarie's mother on the train trip, and for a moment it seems that the innocent Kirsti might give them away. At Uncle Henrik's, the Nazis make a cursory search of the house, only to be fooled because Henrik pretends that his Great-Aunt Birte has died. Even after Ellen and her parents leave for their boat, their escape is still in jeopardy. In their haste to leave the farm, Mr. Rosen has dropped a packet containing a drug-laced handkerchief that was used to temporarily destroy the Nazi dogs' ability to smell. Because Mrs. Johansen has broken her ankle, Annemarie must put her own friendship to a test, traveling through the woods and facing the Nazis alone in order to take the handkerchief to her uncle's boat. Drawing courage from the story of "Little Red Riding Hood," which she has frequently told to Kirsti, Annemarie outwits the Nazis and accomplishes her mission. The Rosens escape to Sweden, and two years later, when the war ends, the Johansens hope that they will see their friends again.

Through helping Ellen escape, Annemarie gradually learns the true meaning of bravery. Early in the novel, she recalls a story her father often tells about a Danish boy who told German soldiers that all Denmark must be the king's bodyguard. Annemarie, however, is not sure whether she could be bold enough to stand up for what she believes. She likes to think that "an ordinary person would never be called upon for courage" (*Number,* 26). In helping the Jews escape from Denmark, Annemarie discovers that ordinary people may indeed be called upon to demonstrate heroism. In the end, it becomes clear that, like the Cowardly Lion in *The Wizard of Oz* (1900), Annemarie has possessed courage all along. Being strong, Uncle Henrik eventually tells Annemarie, does not mean *not* being frightened. Henrik assures her that she is "Fright-ened, but determined, and if the time came to be brave, I am quite sure you would be very, very brave" (*Number,* 76). Annemarie also discovers that sometimes it is easier to be courageous if people do not know the extent of their danger. True bravery means facing difficulties for some-thing you believe in and not thinking about the dangers.

Although *Number the Stars* centers on Annemarie's bravery, it is also about the heroism of an entire nation. According to Annemarie's father, Denmark was not powerful enough to confront the Nazis by raising an army against their invasion. Instead, it will require many acts of individ-ual courage to defeat the invaders. This idea is reinforced by the novel's title, which comes from some Bible verses that Peter Neilsen reads while pretending to mourn Great-Aunt Birte. Apparently by accident, Peter opens the Bible to Psalm 147, which describes how God numbers the stars one by one. The Jews, identified by the novel with Ellen's Star of David necklace, can be saved individually or "one by one." Annemarie does not instantly recognize the meaning of these verses. The idea of counting the stars seems impossible, overwhelming, not unlike the great sea, which she knows frightens Mrs. Rosen. "How could anyone number them one by one, as the psalm said?" Annemarie asks herself. "There were too many. The sky was too big" (*Number,* 87).

Although the value of individual bravery is developed largely through Annemarie's relationship with Ellen, it is reinforced through several important minor characters. Annemarie is able to be brave in her final confrontation with the Nazis by mimicking her younger sister, Kirsti, who is both innocent and fearless, oblivious of the dangers around her. Annemarie also observes the way her parents deal with the Nazis, first, when their apartment is searched, and later when they are questioned on the train ride and at Uncle Henrik's house by the sea. Although Annemarie and Ellen are safe at the end of the novel, Lowry hints at the horrors of war through the subsequent execution of Peter Neilsen and the revelation that Annemarie's older sister, Lise, was killed for working with the Resistance.

As she travels through the woods to Henrik's boat, Annemarie main-tains her courage by acting out the story of "Little Red Riding Hood." This is just one of many references to fairy tales and stories that provide Annemarie with hope and comfort and that contrast with the harsh reality of war. Both Annemarie and Ellen clearly enjoy hearing stories. Early in the novel, the two girls make up their own paper-doll play based on what Mrs. Johansen has related to them from her favorite novel, Margaret Mitchell's *Gone with the Wind*. Ironically, Annemarie is largely unconscious that Mitchell's book is a war story whose heroine survives through determination and bravery that she too must develop.

Annemarie and her mother both relate bedtime fairy tales to Kirsti, who is fascinated with kings and queens. Annemarie herself admits enjoying fairy tales, and Hans Christian Andersen's "Little Mermaid" is a particular favorite. For Annemarie, fairy tales represent a time of innocence and happy endings; they are also one of the few constants in her life. "The whole world had changed," Annemarie muses early in the novel. "Only the fairy tales remained the same" (*Number,* 17). Finding herself making up new fairy tales to please Kirsti, Annemarie discerns a disjunction between these stories and the actuality of the Nazi invasion. Yet, finding herself in the woods, she assumes the heroine's role in "Little Red Riding Hood," carrying a basket to a relative and trying to escape wolves. Although Annemarie recognizes that fairy tales are fiction, their escapism and happy endings also provide hope. By becoming Red Riding Hood, she believes that she can survive her encounter with the Nazi "wolves." After all, she has done it countless times when telling Kirsti the story.

Annemarie's impersonation of Red Riding Hood is only one of many instances in which the novel's characters pretend to be something they are not. Annemarie and Ellen both like to use their imaginations—playing with paper dolls, acting in plays, and telling stories. Under the German occupation, however, playacting is essential to survival. Early in the novel, Annemarie pretends that Kirsti's fish-scale shoes are not ugly, her mother says that Danish naval vessels exploding are really fireworks for Kirsti's birthday, and her father talks in code on the telephone. Later Ellen must pretend to be Lise to prevent detection, and Annemarie mourns a fictional great aunt. Although uncomfortable with the fact that she is helping to perpetuate a lie, Annemarie nevertheless realizes that she is protecting Ellen.

Much of the strength of the novel derives from Lowry's ability to present daily life during World War II in terms that a child can understand. Kirsti's obsession with pink-frosted cupcakes (which are no longer available) and her disgust with fish-scale shoes focus on objects that would be of particular importance to a child. Lowry enlivens the story with other details as well: Annemarie's purchase of a single button, a bicycle with wooden wheels, the burning of Tivoli Gardens, the Nazis' seizure of Henrik's butter. Whereas some readers have criticized the book because it does not dramatize the Nazi death camps that Ellen and her family barely escape, it clearly suggests that a happy ending is sometimes achieved only at great cost. Although Ellen and her family do escape and no harm comes to Annemarie and her parents, Annemarie's own sister and Peter Neilsen are killed by the Nazis; furthermore, two years after Ellen's escape, Annemarie is still waiting, hoping to see her friend, an event that may or may not ever take place. Lowry herself says that in writing the book she was not trying to provide a complete history of the horrors of World War II, and many teachers have written to her, praising the novel because it is an excellent introduction to the topic for young readers (Chaston 1994).

In her Newbery Acceptance Speech, Lowry argues that she cannot write about "huge events." If she were a newspaper reporter covering a catastrophe, she would likely "write about a broken lunch box shattered in a puddle" ("Newbery 1990," 416). She goes on to quote W. H. Auden's poem *Musée des Beaux Arts,* which describes Brueghel's painting *The Fall of Icarus.* Both the poem and the painting tell "of children on a pond, skating, not noticing that a horrifying thing is happening in the sky" ("Newbery 1990," 417). Lowry explains that the subject of *Number the Stars* was too huge, that she could not cover it all. She "could only write about the child who skates on the pond at the edge of events. The day-to-day life of a child in that place, at that time" ("Newbery 1990," 417).

To make the events of the war accessible to young readers, Lowry utilizes simple, direct language and a concise structure that imitates the very stories that Annemarie tells Kirsti. The incidents in the book are alternately suspenseful and humorous. The action of *Number the Stars* is framed by five separate encounters with Nazi soldiers. In the first of these, Annemarie, Ellen, and Kirsti meet the Nazis on a street near their building. Although frightened, Annemarie does most of the talking, yet does not realize how much of a threat the soldiers are. Next the Nazis search Annemarie's home for the Rosens and are put off the track by her father's quick thinking. On the train to Uncle Henrik's house and then in his living room as they pretend to mourn the imaginary Great-Aunt Birte, Annemarie and her family are again questioned by soldiers. Both times, however, Annemarie's mother saves them. Each of these four encounters is increasingly perilous as the soldiers come closer and closer to discovering the truth about the Rosens' escape. In Annemarie's final meeting with the soldiers, one that parallels the first scene in the novel, she again encounters dangers running down a road. This time no one else can rescue her. Because of her mother's broken ankle, Annemarie must take on adult responsibilities. From her previous experiences, however, she has observed the bravery of others and can now emulate them.

Many of the major themes of *Number the Stars* are reinforced by objects and characters that have important symbolic meaning. One extremely important object is Ellen's Star of David necklace, a traditional symbol of Judaism. When the Nazis burst into the Johansen home in the middle of the night, Annemarie rips the necklace from around Ellen's neck and clenches it in her hand to protect her friend. The ornament leaves a mark in Annemarie's palm, a combination of both traditional Christian and Jewish symbols (a wound in the palm and the Star of David), which also represents Annemarie's commitment to helping Ellen. When the war is over, Annemarie wears the necklace to symbolize her friendship with Ellen and the hope that she will return home soon. Other symbolic devices are the pink-frosted cupcakes, which, to Kirsti, represent life before the war, and the Nazis' shiny boots, suggesting the invaders' impersonality and power.

Number the Stars was met with widespread critical acclaim. Mary M. Burns in *Horn Book* noted that the book was "scaled to the comprehension of elementary school readers without sacrificing elements of style." Praising the book as "seamless, compelling, memorable—impossible to forget," she further states that the "limited omniscient third-person perspective . . . draws the reader into the intensity of the situation as a child Annemarie's age might perceive it."[12] Denise Wilms writes that the strength of the novel "lies in its evocation of a deep friendship between two girls and of a caring family who make a profoundly moral choice to protect others during wartime."[13]

Some reviewers seem to want the novel to focus more directly on the horrors of death camps and the violence of war, as in other recent books about the war, such as Robert Innocenti's *Rose Blanche* (1985) and Jane Yolen's *Devil's Arithmetic* (1988) and *Briar Rose* (1992). In *Rose Blanche*, another young girl, like Red Riding Hood, journeys through the woods, taking food to children in a concentration camp. Unlike Annemarie, however, Rose Blanche is shot for her efforts. *The Devil's Arithmetic* and *Briar Rose* make similar use of fairy-tale motifs to paint the brutality and horror of life in the camps. In an article in the *New York Times Book Review*, Edith Milton argues that Annemarie's innocent viewpoint "keeps us at too great a distance to see clearly either the scale of evil or the magnitude of the courage from which this story springs."[14]

Although Lowry does not consider *Number the Stars* as a "Holocaust" book, it is similar in theme to a number of books about World War II.

The Danish underground has been the subject of several other novels, including Nathaniel Benchley's *Bright Candles: A Novel of the Danish Resistance* (1974). Nonfiction books such as Anne Frank's *The Diary of a Young Girl* (1952) and Johanna Reiss's *The Upstairs Room* (1972), as well as fictionalized biographies and novels like Claire Hutchet Bishop's *Twenty and Ten* (1952), Malka Drucker and Michael Halperin's *Jacob's Rescue: A Holocaust Story* (1993), and Carol Matas's *Daniel's Story* (1993) all feature Jewish children who are hidden and protected by Christians.

Number the Stars is a readable and extremely powerful book, certainly worthy of the many honors it has received. It lives up to a wish Lowry expresses in her afterword. In composing the novel, Lowry was moved by a letter written by Kim Malthe-Brunn, a member of the Danish Resistance, who, like Peter Neilsen, was executed. He urged his mother to remember the dream of creating "an ideal human decency, and not a narrow-minded and prejudiced one" (*Number,* 137). Lowry goes on to express the hope that her "story of Denmark, and its people, will remind us all that such a world is possible" (*Number,* 137). In telling Anne-marie's and Ellen's story, Lowry has succeeded in her goal.

The Giver (1993)

Whereas *Number the Stars* is set in the past, Lowry's other Newbery-Award-winning novel takes place in the future. Despite diverse settings and the fact that *Number the Stars* is based on real historical events and *The Giver* is science fiction, the two books deal with very similar themes. The community described in *The Giver* is in its own way every bit as repressive as Nazi-occupied Scandinavia. Indeed, one might view *The Giver* as Lowry's response to those who criticize *Number the Stars* for "skating around the edge" of the holocaust. Although disguised as a futuristic Utopia, Jonas's community, like the Third Reich, uses language and rules to condition its members to accept the extermination of those who are different.

In creating *The Giver*, Lowry has drawn on a number of her own memories. In her Newbery Acceptance Speech, she talks about living in a close-knit Americanized community in Japan that effectively blocked out interactions with the local culture. As a curious 11-year-old, Lowry would ride her bicycle into the real Japan, the equivalent of "Elsewhere," the name given for the world outside the community in *The Giver*. Lowry then mentions several other events that helped shape the novel: the way the girls in her college dormitory shut out one who seemed different; her son Grey's wedding to a German girl, an event that made the inhabitants of two countries "one people"; and her interview with Carl Nelson, the painter who went blind. Toward the end of Lowry's speech, she mentions a woman who once asked her, "Why do we have to tell this Holocaust thing over and over? Is it really *necessary?* ("Newbery 1994," 418). According to Lowry's German daughter-in-law, the story must be told so that we do not forget it. All of these events, Lowry explains, are tributaries "into the river of thought that will create *The Giver*" ("Newbery 1994," 418).

In her Acceptance Speech, Lowry also describes how, at the time she was writing the novel, her father had lost much of his memory. As mentioned earlier, Lowry's father and mother were in the same rest home. Her mother, who was dying, was full of stories and memories that she wanted to share with her daughter, whereas her father could not even remember her dead sister, Helen (Chaston 1994). A more general concern also influenced the writing of this novel. Lowry is interested in the loss of diversity in the world. In her travels, she has discovered that the world is moving toward "sameness." Both people and places seem to be losing their individuality ("Trumpet II").

When Lowry began to write the novel, she tried to create a real utopia. "It was only after I began writing," Lowry explains, "that I began to see the dark side of this ideal world" ("Trumpet II"). Concerned that the world she was creating might not be clear, Lowry, who does not usually share her drafts with anyone, had her friend Martin Small and her oldest daughter, Alix, read the manuscript as she was writing it (Chaston 1994). The Children's Literature Research Collection at the University of Minnesota contains two manuscript versions of *The Giver* and letters from Lowry's editor and his assistants who made suggestions for revision. Even in the original version, everyone at Houghton Mifflin was fascinated with the story, but the complexity of creating a futuristic society required a few modifications. Most of these were cosmetic, including elimination of some inadvertent references to color (since the members of the community see no colors) and minor changes in some of the scenes where Jonas receives The Giver's memories.[15]

The protagonist of *The Giver* is an introspective and sensitive 12-year-old boy named Jonas, who is concerned with finding his niche in society. Jonas belongs to "the community," an isolated group cut off from the outside world, which is referred to as "Elsewhere." At first glance, the community does not seem all that different from our present world, despite clues that the novel probably takes place a couple of hundred years in the future. The community includes houses, schools, a child-care center, and a rest home. Jonas enjoys riding his bicycle, argues with his sister, Lily, and wants to fit in. He is also becoming attracted to the opposite sex, in particular to a girl named Fiona.

To some, Jonas's community might seem like the ideal society. There are no single-parent families, the elderly receive special care, and children show respect for their teachers. There is evidently no war, disease, hunger, poverty, or lasting pain. Bad weather has been eliminated, as has anything that might make members of the community uncomfortable. No one seems to worry about being safe, and everyone knows everyone else. In addition, the society seems to value men and women equally, and stereotypical gender roles have evidently disappeared. In Jonas's own family, his mother holds a prominent position in the Department of Justice, while his father is a Nurturer, tending newborn infants in a special care center. Indeed, sexual desire is also controlled by pills that all citizens take once they have reached puberty. Since the citizens of the community have been conditioned not to see colors, there are no apparent racial divisions.

Everyone in the community has the opportunity to work and is provided with appropriate training. At the age of 12, all children are considered adults and receive an "Assignment," or life's work. At an annual ceremony, after careful deliberation by the Elders, the "Twelves" are assigned to such jobs as "Fish Hatchery Attendant," "Instructor," "Pilot," "Nurturer," or "Assistant Director of Recreation." One of the least prestigious jobs is "Birthmother," and, it turns out, only a few people actually give birth to children. Infants are assigned to appropriate "fathers" and "mothers" when the children turn one.

Despite the appearance of tolerance and flexibility, the society follows very rigid rules that are constantly blurted out over loudspeakers. Language, which must be very precise, is a means of controlling inappropriate ideas. School children have a very specific routine. Indeed, Lily becomes quite upset when a visitor from another community appears unfamiliar with the rules.

At the same time, a number of fairly ordinary aspects of contemporary life have been eliminated or altered. Animals apparently have disappeared, and there are no songs. The only books are those hidden in the dwelling of the "Receiver of Memory," the only citizen who possesses knowledge of what life was like before the community began.

When it becomes time for Jonas to receive his assignment, the woman in charge of the ceremony skips over him. After the rest of the

Twelves receive their assignments, it is announced that Jonas has not been "assigned," he has been "selected." He is to become the next Receiver of Memory. Because Jonas has intelligence, integrity, and courage, he has been unanimously chosen for this special duty. One of the talents that qualifies Jonas for this task is the "Capacity to See Beyond," the ability to occasionally see color in his black-and-white world.[16] An attempt 10 years earlier at training a new Receiver of Memory had failed, and the committee of Elders has put a lot of care into selecting a new Receiver.

Jonas now finds himself undergoing special training with the old Receiver of Memory, an elderly man he calls "The Giver." Jonas soon learns that The Giver lives an isolated life and that his function has been to provide the community with help when decisions need to be made. This is possible because he has been somewhat mystically endowed with memories of war, pain, joy, color, light, and music, all from a time before the community was created. In order for Jonas to take his place, The Giver must transmit to him "the memories of the whole world. . . . Before you, before me, before the previous Receiver, and generations before him" (*Giver,* 77).

Jonas is shocked to discover that The Giver is quite cynical about the community. As he tells Jonas, when their people "made the choice to go to Sameness," they "gained control of many things" but "had to let go of others" (95). Like The Giver, Jonas also comes to the conclusion that the community should not have given up control of things such as color and music. Eventually Jonas learns that The Giver's own daughter, Rosemary, has previously had Jonas's assignment, and because of the pain it involved and her new understanding of the community, she asked to be "released."

As Jonas's training continues, The Giver begins to transmit some of his memories to Jonas. The first such memory is of "snow." As Jonas receives this memory, it is as if he is literally riding a sled down a snowy hill. For Jonas, snow, hills, and sleds are all new; none of them exist in his community. Jonas also begins to see color in the world around him, first red, followed by the colors of the rainbow, and he becomes angry that his "groupmates" are "satisfied with their lives which had none of the brilliance his own was taking on" (*Giver,* 99).

Not all of the memories that Jonas receives from The Giver are pleasant. One day Jonas experiences a violent elephant hunt. Later he is given the memory of another sled ride, only in this one he is thrown from the sled and breaks a leg, resulting in real-life pain, something that the other citizens rarely, if ever, feel. This unpleasant experience is followed by the memory of a war battle in which Jonas sees young boys and horses dying around him. To counterbalance the horror of this particular recollection, The Giver gives Jonas good memories for a while: a birthday party, a trip to an art museum, and then The Giver's favorite memory, which involves a family opening presents around what is evidently a Christmas tree.

As the novel continues, Jonas comes to realize how much his society has given up. Privy to information that no other citizen has because of his new role, Jonas finds himself questioning the world in which he has been raised. Why are there no grandparents, no colors? Why is there no snow? Then he discovers the community's most awful secret. Through The Giver's closed-circuit television, Jonas learns that when individuals are released, they are actually executed by a lethal injection. Members of the community are released for breaking rules, for becoming too old, or for not conforming.

None of the other members of the community completely understand the nature of the releases or even question the practice. Instead they blindly follow the community's dictates. For example, Jonas's nurturing father routinely helps in the release of infants. In one case, twins are deemed too confusing, so the weaker one is released. Because of the privileges that The Receiver of Memory enjoys, Jonas has the chance to secretly observe his father injecting the twin with poison, noting that he smiles cheerfully while dispensing death. Another infant, Gabriel, is threatened with release because he does not sleep through the night even though he is approaching the age of two. Jonas's friend Fiona is assigned to care for the elderly in the House of the Old and will soon be willingly involved in their releases. Jonas's mother is very practical, an important member of the Department of Justice, and has ruled that a man who has broken the law three times must be released. Jonas's sister, Lily, acts like many typical community children although there is no doubt that she will eventually be conditioned to accept the rules of her society.

Having received some of The Giver's memories of the past, Jonas recognizes what his society has lost. Like his father, Jonas has a nurturing side and comes to care for the infant Gabriel, who is temporarily under the care of Jonas's family because he cannot sleep through the night. When Jonas learns that Gabriel is scheduled for execution, he decides he must make his escape immediately and, without even talking to The Giver, rides out of the community on a bicycle, carrying Gabriel with him in an attempt to save himself and the baby and to find answers "Elsewhere," in the outside world. The Giver, too, realizes what the community has given up to maintain its way of life and plans to help Jonas escape. As a result of his flight, Jonas's memories supposedly will be transmitted to the other citizens, allowing them to experience joy and pain.

After leaving the community, Jonas and Gabriel travel for many days. Soon they encounter snow, which Jonas knows only through The Giver's memories. The two children are tired, cold, and hungry but continue on their journey by foot. To comfort Gabriel, Jonas shares memories of sunlight and warmth with the child. Just when Jonas feels he can go no further, he finds a sled on the top of a hill, exactly like the one in the first memory he received from The Giver. Like Elizabeth and Charles in *Autumn Street*, who also ride a sled to the end of the woods, Jonas and Gabriel sail away on the sled toward Elsewhere. As the novel ends, Jonas hears music and people singing, not unlike another of The Giver's memories. The novel closes, "Behind him, across vast distances of space and time, from the place he had left, he thought he heard music, too. But perhaps it was only an echo" (*Giver,* 180).

The novel's ending is intentionally ambiguous, leaving the reader to ponder whether the red, yellow, and blue lights on the trees that Jonas sees are real or whether they are only memories he has received from The Giver. In her Newbery Acceptance speech, Lowry has described some of the ways in which her readers have interpreted the novel's ending. One sixth grader wrote to suggest that Jonas and Gabriel "were traveling in a circle. When they came to 'Elsewhere' it was their old community, but they had accepted the memories and all the feelings that go along with it" ("Newbery 1994," 420). Another child suggested that Jonas was like Jesus because he took on himself the pain of the whole community and that Elsewhere was like heaven. Yet another argued that Jonas and Gabriel had made it back to the past. One seventh-grade boy felt that the final episode "was a bummer" because the children just died at the end. Most children, Lowry explains, "have perceived the magic of the circular journey" ("Newbery 1994," 421). Both in her Newbery speech and in personal interviews, Lowry refuses to interpret the ending, allowing her readers to choose the one they like best.

Even the written comments from the staff at Houghton Mifflin who read the original manuscript suggest multiple interpretations of the novel's conclusion. A letter to Lowry from her editor assumes that the first memory that Jonas receives from The Giver comes back to kill him. However, a somewhat later communication says that her editor and readers think the ending means that Jonas has found a sympathetic society and that memories will now endure ("Giver Manuscript").

The novel is written in an accessible, almost journalistic, prose that contrasts with the intense, lyrical descriptions of the memories that Jonas begins to receive from The Giver. Writing in the *New York Times*, Karen Ray has described the novel's style as "appropriately flat yet expressive."[17] A gripping novel, *The Giver* holds the reader's attention to the very end. The most powerful part of the book is the ending, in which fact and fiction, the present and memory blend together as Jonas struggles to bring Gabriel safely to the outside world that, so far, exists for him only in the memories he has received from The Giver.

The Giver, which takes place from one December to the next, has a mythic, almost allegorical, quality, one quite different from Lowry's comical, contemporary family stories. Some of her other books, notably *Number the Stars*, draw on fairy-tale allusions and structure to tell realistic stories. Although *The Giver* makes no direct references to fairy tales, the opening has a once-upon-a-time quality. The joys of the outside world, especially the memory of sledding down a hill and a family celebrating Christmas, become Jonas's fairy tales, ones that sustain him in his trials. In an interview with Walter Lorraine, Lowry has noted the similarities between the ending of this novel and Annemarie's trip through the woods in *Number the Stars*. According to Lowry, both Jonas and Annemarie make their treacherous journeys to change their world in some way and overcome their fears by calling on stories. Annemarie is sustained by the story of "Little Red Riding Hood." Jonas comforts himself with The Giver's memories, which are his stories ("Trumpet II").

Although Lowry was not conscious of their particular meanings, the mythic quality of *The Giver* is further supported by her choice of the characters' names. *Jonas* is a variant of *Jonah,* the name of the reluctant Old Testament prophet who was called to save the land of Ninevah and who was swallowed by a great fish. In the New Testament, Jesus refers to the "sign of Jonah" as a foreshadowing of his own death and resurrection. The name *Jonah* is frequently interpreted as *the dove.* The choice of this particular name lends weight to those who choose to interpret the ending as a religious allegory. The infant Gabriel shares a name with another Biblical figure, the angel who was sent to Daniel in the Old Testament and then to both Zacharias and Mary in the Book of Luke. Another suggestive name is that of The Giver's daughter, Rosemary, which, according to an English rhyme, stands for remembrance, surely an appropriate appellation for a child of the Receiver of Memory.

The Giver treats a number of important social concerns and as a result deals with some sensitive issues. As is the case with many dystopian novels, the book argues against blind obedience to society's rules and dictates. In this novel, the main character's only solution to the ethical problems he encounters is to run away. The novel suggests how language can be used to condition people to accept atrocities and argues that there are problems that result from trying to eradicate individual differences. As a result, the community has eliminated the freedom to make choices. Creating a society in which no one feels pain is, in actuality, destructive and leads to the devaluation of individuality.

In order for Jonas to feel compelled to leave the community, Lowry must show his horror at the way his society complacently condones murder. Thus Jonas witnesses his father happily following orders, killing a baby. Another potentially controversial aspect of the society is that physical love has been eradicated—members of the community take pills that eliminate all sexual desire.

Repressive, nightmarish future societies (extolled by their leaders as the perfect way of life) have been the subject of a number of dystopian novels regularly read by young adults and taught in high schools. Both Aldous Huxley's *Brave New World* (1933) and Ray Bradbury's *Fahrenheit 451* (1953) portray future worlds whose citizens are assigned specific social roles, much like the members of the community in *The Giver*. In all three of these worlds, art, music, and literature have been systematically purged and often replaced by technology or more "practical" pursuits. In George Orwell's well-known *1984* (1940), "Big Brother" and the "Thought Police" monitor people's actions and ideas, much like the rasping voice that spews out commands in Lowry's book. More important, in both *1984* and *The Giver*, language is used as a way to manipulate and control people's thoughts.

The Giver also has specific similarities to two short stories that may have helped inspire it. In "Funes, the Memorious" (1961) by Jorge Luis Borges, a man is burdened with remembering everything that has ever happened to him in great detail.[18] This is a story that, Lowry recalls, she asked her editor to read a number of years ago (Chaston 1994). The destructive nature of Funes's memory and his statement that "I have more memories in myself alone than all men have had since the world was a world" surely conjure up the character of The Giver (Borges, 40). Another well-known story, Ursula K. Le Guin's "The Ones Who Walk Away from

Omelas" (1973), treats an apparently ideal society whose members' "happiness, the beauty of their city, the tenderness of their friendships, the health of their children, the wisdom of their scholars, the skill of their makers, even of the abundance of their harvest and the kindly weathers of their skies" are contingent on one child's being imprisoned and living in "abominable misery."[19] When young people grow up and learn about this secret, there are some who simply walk away from the society, unwilling to accept that their happiness is achieved through the pain of others. According to Le Guin, the place they go is indescribable, and it "is possible that it does not exist" (Le Guin, 284).

Dystopian novels written specifically for young adults are not new. Two notable examples are John Christopher's *White Mountains* (1967), in which people's actions are controlled by alien beings and its protagonists must flee to the "Elsewhere" provided by the Swiss Alps, and Madeleine L'Engle's *A Wrinkle in Time* (1962), whose climax takes place on the planet Camazotz, where everyone is expected to conform. One reviewer has also argued that the end of *The Giver* reworks Hans Christian Andersen's story "The Little Match Girl," whose main character draws warmth from images of family and Christmas before freezing to death, not unlike one possible reading of *The Giver*'s ending.[20]

Although reviewers have commented on how different it is from Lowry's other novels, *The Giver* actually reworks a number of her favorite themes. As mentioned earlier, in the comical *Anastasia Krupnik* (1979), a young girl learns the importance of memory and, as in *The Giver*, learns that obtaining "the inward eye" is accompanied by suffering. At the end of *The Giver*, Jonas must leave the family that has been artificially created for him, much like Rabble and her mother in Lowry's *Rabble Starkey*. As previously noted, *The Giver* can also be seen as expanding on the themes of Lowry's other Newbery-Award-winning book, *Number the Stars* (1990), which deals with an act of heroism. The protagonists of both books learn much about the meaning of fear and the fact that they must ultimately risk their lives for those they care about. At the same time, in both *Number the Stars* and *The Giver*, euphemisms help to soften acts of violence.

Of all of Lowry's novels, *The Giver* has received the most attention. *The Giver* was published to critical acclaim, particularly from the *Horn Book*, which printed the editorial by Anita Silvey. A review of the novel by Ann A. Flowers in the same issue calls the book "skillfully written" and suggests that "the air of disquiet is delicately insinuated."[21] The

Horn Book continued its celebration of *The Giver* through a November/December column by Patty Campbell, who writes that the book is one of those that "takes hardened young-adult reviewers by surprise" and that it is "a book so unlike what has gone before, so rich in levels of meaning, so daring in complexity of symbol and metaphor, so challenging in the ambiguity of its conclusion, that we are left with all our neat little everyday categories and judgments hanging useless." Campbell compares *The Giver* to books such as Robert Cormier's *I Am the Cheese* and Terry Davis's *Mysterious Ways.* For Campbell, the book represents a leap forward for Lowry "in mastering the creation of a subtext by innuendo, foreshadowing, and resonance."[22] With such positive early press, it is not surprising that in 1994 *The Giver* earned Lowry her second Newbery Prize. In addition to the Newbery Award, the book has received the Regina Medal, the Pacific Northwest Library Association's Young Readers' Choice Award, the Rebecca Caudill Young Readers' Book Award (Illinois), the Sequoyah Book Award (Oklahoma), and a *Boston Globe-Horn Book* honor citation. It has also been named an American Library Association Best Book for Young Adults, an American Library Association Notable Book for Children, a *School Library Journal* Best Book of the Year, and a *Booklist* Editor's Choice.

The Giver is a suspenseful story with a gripping and controversial ending, one that will sustain the interest of young adult readers. It also deals with important social issues, including the value of the individual, the importance of remembering the past, the dangers of personal manipulation through language and social conditioning, and the need for both color and music. *The Giver* also compares favorably to a number of important adult books that use future societies to question an apparent devaluation of the individual in our present culture. At the same time, it is accessible to younger readers, and its ending prompts thought-provoking discussion.

Rabble Starkey, Number the Stars, and *The Giver*—each in their own way—demonstrate Lowry's ability to stretch and experiment while continuing to explore favorite themes, including memories, friendship, and home. The strong voice of the narrator in *Rabble Starkey,* the deceptively simple prose of *Number the Stars,* and the almost allegorical tone of *The Giver* demonstrate Lowry's ability to write in a variety of styles and in a number of fictional genres. The almost universal commendation these books have received clearly establishes Lowry as one of the most important American children's writers of the twentieth century.

Chapter Seven

A Growing Reputation

When Lois Lowry's first novel, *A Summer to Die*, won the International Reading Association's Children's Book Award, it seemed clear that Lowry would become a successful children's writer. Few would have guessed, however, that she would go on to produce 23 novels for children and young adults, winning award after award, and that her novels would become part of the curriculum of schools around the world. The many children's choice book awards Lowry has won and the fact that all of her novels are currently in print attest to this popularity. Several of her books, including *Number the Stars* and *The Giver*, have been best sellers among children's books. In fact, in 1995 both of these books were simultaneously on the *New York Times* list of best-selling "Chapter Books."[1] In July of 1995 *Publisher's Weekly* listed *The Giver* as the number one best-selling children's novel, beating out novel versions of two popular 1995 children's films, *The Indian in the Cupboard* and *Pocahontas*.[2] Lowry's books have been published in a variety of languages (although *Number the Stars* has yet to be translated into German), and they are particularly well known in Australia and New Zealand.

As I have already mentioned, both *Find a Stranger, Say Goodbye* and *Taking Care of Terrific* have been made into short films for television. Lowry continues to receive offers from filmmakers who are interested in adapting her works. She has resisted offers to make the Anastasia books into a television series, but Portabello Productions (a British company) currently has the rights to *Number the Stars,* and Jeff Bridges, ASIS Productions, and Lancit Productions have contracted to coproduce a film based on *The Giver*. *Number the Stars* has sparked at least two adaptations for the stage. In 1994 a group of children in Pullyup, Washington, mounted a production of "Friends Forever," a play written by a 10-year-old girl based on *Number the Stars*.[3] The following year Apple Tree's Theatre for Young People, located near Chicago, presented its own dramatization, which the *Chicago Tribune* described as "emotionally charged," offering "a moving testimony to the bravery of common people of all ages and the power of solidarity."[4]

Despite their popularity and the many awards they have received, Lowry's work has gained widespread critical attention only in the last few years. Even today Lowry is still asked when she will write a "real book," now that she has had so much success writing for young people. On one occasion Lowry responded, "Would you ask a pediatrician why she didn't become a real doctor?" (Mehren, 3) For some scholars, the popularity of the Anastasia series has garnered her a reputation as a writer of humorous books, a genre sometimes overlooked in literary circles.

In the 1980s, with the popularity of her first books for children and a growing interest in children's literature as a field of academic study, Lowry became the subject of several published interviews intended primarily for teachers and librarians. Two of the first such interviews appeared in *Contemporary Authors* (1984) and *Publisher's Weekly* (1986). Both of these explore Lowry's early career and the creation of the character, Anastasia Krupnik. In 1985 Houghton Mifflin produced a videotape interview with Lowry that is still available. These interviews have been followed by countless others in sources as varied as *Authors and Artists for Young People* (1990), The Trumpet Club's "Author Study Tapes Series" (1990, 1994), and *Listen to Their Voices: Twenty Interviews with Women Who Write* (1993). In 1994, after receiving her second Newbery Award, Lowry was interviewed in the *Los Angeles Times*, the *Boston Sunday Herald*, and the *Reading Teacher*. In 1995 The Learning Works published a biography of Lowry for young readers written by a writer of children's nonfiction, Lois Markham. According to one interview, Lowry is "occasionally stunned to find herself in the company of famous authors whose lives are dissected down to the designs of their kitchens" (Mehren, 3).

During this same period Lowry began to attract the attention of critics of children's literature. In 1986 Laura Zaidman's detailed survey of Lowry's work appeared in *Dictionary of Literary Biography*. At that time Zaidman suggested that Lowry's success comes from "her clear writing, delightful humor, intriguing characters, and memorable stories with universal values" (Zaidman, 261). The following year Eric Kimmel's "Anastasia Agonistes: The Tragicomedy of Lois Lowry," published in *Horn Book*, was the first serious look at the Anastasia series. Kimmel argues that no other writer of children's literature "wears both comic and tragic masks as well as Lois Lowry" (Kimmel, 182). He goes on to argue that Lowry's humor, like that of Mark Twain, grows out of her awareness of the darker side of life.

Especially with the publication of *Number the Stars* and *The Giver* and their subsequent Newbery awards, interest in Lowry's works has increased. In a 1994 session of the International Children's Literature Association held in Durham, New Hampshire, four different papers focused on Lowry's books.[5] In my own survey of American children's literature of the 1980s, published in *Children's Literature in Education*, I include *Rabble Starkey* and *Number the Stars* in my own list of "Honor Books 1980–1990," citing Lowry and Beverly Cleary as "established writers" who, during the 1980s, "experimented with topics as well as forms new to them."[6] In 1995 Michael Cart included a lengthy discussion of the Anastasia series in *What's So Funny? Wit and Humor in American Children's Literature*.

This increased critical attention to Lowry's books has resulted in part from their adoption into the curriculum of schools around the world. Articles in *Horn Book* (1993), the *Instructor* (1994), *Beacham's Guide to Young Adult Literature* (1994), *Adolescent Literature as a Complement to the Classics, Volume II* (1995), as well as teaching guides such as my own *Literature Guide to Lois Lowry's Number the Stars* (1993), all affirm the pedagogical popularity of Lowry's work, especially *Number the Stars* and *The Giver*. A 1994 article in the *Herald* (Glasgow, Scotland) describes how a holocaust unit, featuring both *Number the Stars* and Anne Frank's *Diary of a Young Girl* (1947), has been created for use with second- or third-year Scottish high school students.[7]

With the integration of Lowry's novels into the curriculum of various schools, they have on occasion become the subject of a few censorship debates. In a January 29, 1985, guest column in the *Star-Tribune* (Casper, Wyoming), Dave and Danna Pedry, whose nine-year-old daughter attended the Natrona County school system, cited *Anastasia Krupnik* and *Anastasia Again!*, as well as two books by Judy Blume, as being "filthy, profane" and "as pornographic as *Playboy* is for adults." The authors attack Lowry's books because they supposedly "indulge feelings of hatred," an "anti-life attitude," "anti-religious mentality," "profanity," and because characters read *Playboy* and *Cosmopolitan*.[8] The Pedrys' attempt to have these books banned, based on an exaggeration of minor details in the first Anastasia books, was ultimately unsuccessful.

Because of the novel's almost immediate integration into the curriculum of schools across the country, *The Giver* has also been the subject of various censorship attacks. A 1994 article by Janus Adams in *Ms.* magazine maintains that the novel is sexist and racist, arguing that the Giver has refused to give his own daughter his memories and that he plans on being taken care of by her in his old age. The same article also criticizes the book because "the figure of the African oral historian, the griot, as holder of memory-in-mind and relayer of divine wisdom and guidance is supplanted by a white man."[9] Unfortunately, Adams has not read the book carefully because the Giver does choose to pass on memories to his daughter, who is now dead, and there are no distinguishable races whatsoever in the community. Such divisions have been eradicated.

In 1995 *The Giver* appeared on a list made up by People for the American Way of the 10 books most frequently the subject of censorship debates during that year. One attempt to censor the book occurred in September of 1995, when a mother from Indianapolis wrote a letter to the *Indianapolis Star* questioning the judgment of a school system that would make the novel required reading in her daughter's seventh-grade English class. "This book made me feel depressed and sick," the woman wrote.[10] The letter was met with a number of responses suggesting that the woman had missed the point of the novel. A ninth-grade English teacher who was using the novel as part of the curriculum wrote that she hoped the book would stir up and encourage readers to hold onto their "freedoms and rights, as well as those of the elderly, the handicapped and the unborn."[11] Another mother wrote in describing how she and her husband and sixth-grade son read the book together. She found *The Giver* "a beautiful, thought provoking book that asks children to consider if we should solve society's problems at the cost of our humanity."[12]

According to Lowry, her continued popularity and the many awards she has received have not changed her. Instead, awards such as her two Newbery Medals provide "affirmation; it makes you feel as if you're doing the right thing for you" (Chaston 1994). Lowry continues to look to the future, working on a number of projects. She promises that there are more books to come about Anastasia and Sam and possibly a novel for adults.

Few authors of books for children and young adults have managed to maintain such a large readership and please the literary critics as well as Lois Lowry. Her diverse subjects, which Lowry treats with wit and pathos, have earned her an important place in twentieth-century children's literature. As I have suggested, one key ingredient has been Lowry's ability to remember the experience of being a child and to reach her readers with her "inward eye." In a 1991 speech Lowry talks about this special ability, discussing the response *Number the Stars* has received from her readers. Children who write to her say that in reading this particular book, one that remembers a past and a place that seem distant to them, "they enter that magic realm which a book can provide for both writer and reader. It becomes real. It becomes a place they can go to. It is a dangerous place, and they enter it with fear; but they emerge from it with honor" ("Pennsylvania," 20). Whether Lowry is transporting her readers to the woods at the end of Autumn Street, the streets of Copenhagen, a small town in Virginia, or a futuristic community, she indeed manages to make the settings of her books and the characters of her stories real. In the speech just cited, Lowry quotes a line from *Us and Uncle Fraud*: "[We] changed in our knowledge of things" (*Fraud,* 147). Lowry explains that this quote represents the real "magic that happens in writing out of memories, out of one's childhood awareness. In looking back . . . I changed in my knowledge of things" ("Pennsylvania," 20). Lowry's books have the ability to change her young readers' knowledge of things, helping them gain the "inward eye" that Anastasia Krupnik tries so hard to obtain.

Notes and References

Chapter One

1. Lois Lowry, *Anastasia Krupnik* (Boston: Houghton, 1979), 72; hereafter cited in text as *Anastasia*.
2. Joel D. Chaston, personal interview with Lois Lowry on October 6, 1994, in Cambridge, Massachusetts; hereafter cited in text. Factual material in this chapter that is not otherwise documented comes from this interview.
3. Lowry is not sure whether Carl Hammersberg himself was born in the United States or in Norway (Chaston, 1994).
4. Dieter Miller, "Lois Lowry," in *Authors and Artists for Young People,* vol. 5 , ed. Agnes Garrett and Helga P. McCue (Detroit: Gale, 1990), 130; hereafter cited in text.
5. Lois Lowry, "Lois Lowry," in *Something about the Author Autobiographical Series,* vol. 3, ed. Adele Sarkissian (Detroit: Gale, 1986), 137; hereafter cited in text as "Lois Lowry."
6. Lois Lowry, "The Recital," *Philadelphia* 68 (December 1977): 118; hereafter cited in text as "Recital."
7. Jean Ross, "Lois Lowry," in *Contemporary Authors, New Revision Series,* vol. 13 (Detroit: Gale, 1984), 333; hereafter cited in text.
8. Walter Lorraine, "Lois Lowry: Author Study Tape." Holmes, Pa.: Trumpet Club, 1994, audiocassette; hereafter cited in text as "Trumpet II."
9. Lois Lowry, "Introduction," in *Dear Author: Students Write about the Books that Changed Their Lives, Collected by Weekly Reader Magazine* (Berkeley, Calif.: Conari, 1995), ix, xii; hereafter cited in text as *Author.*
10. Lois Lowry, "Afterword," in *Pollyanna* by Eleanor H. Porter (1913; reprint, New York: Dell, 1986), 219.
11. Alice Cary, "And They All Lived . . . Ever After," *Boston Sunday Herald, People* supplement, June 26, 1994, 7; hereafter cited in text.
12. Lois Lowry, "Remembering How It Was," *Writer* (July 1987): 16–19.
13. Whereas Lowry's stepgrandmother, who appears in *Autumn Street,* was a staunch Episcopalian, her grandfather was a Presbyterian.
14. Lois Lowry, "Newbery Medal Acceptance," *Horn Book* 70 (1994): 15; hereafter cited in text as "Newbery 1994."
15. Lois Lowry, "How Does It Feel to Be on a TV Quiz Show? Don't Ask." *New York Times,* March 31, 1974, Section 2, 23.
16. Lois Lowry, "A Visit with Lois Lowry." (Boston: Houghton, 1985, videotape); hereafter cited in text as "Visit."

17. Elizabeth Mehren, "Author Lois Lowry Never Planned to Write Fiction for Adults, but Fate and a Natural Connection to Her Audience Stepped in," *Los Angeles Times, Life and Style,* November 9, 1994, 3; hereafter cited in text.

18. Mickey Pearlman, *Listen to Their Voices: Twenty Interviews with Women Who Write* (New York: Norton, 1992), 174; hereafter cited in text.

19. Amanda Smith, *"PW* Interviews Lois Lowry," *Publisher's Weekly* 21 (February 1986): 152; hereafter cited in text.

20. Marjorie Lewis, "Find a Stranger, Say Goodbye," *School Library Journal* (May 1978): 78.

21. Bill Van Siclen, "Children's Book Festival: Off to Meet the Literary Wizards," *The Providence Journal-Bulletin,* October 21, 1994, 1D.

22. See Judith Saltman, *The Riverside Anthology of Children's Literature,* 6th ed. (Boston: Houghton, 1985), 729–31.

23. George Nicholson, "Lois Lowry: Authors on Tape." (Holmes, Penn.: Trumpet Club, 1990, audiocassette); hereafter cited in text as "Trumpet I."

24. Laura Zaidman, "Lois Lowry," in *Dictionary of Literary Biography, Vol. 52: American Writers for Children Since 1960—Fiction,* ed. Glenn E. Estes (Detroit: Gale, 1986), 256; hereafter cited in text.

25. Lois Lowry, Letter to Joel Chaston, December 19, 1996; hereafter cited in text as "Letter."

26. Lois Lowry, "Stories Behind the Stories," in *Where Do You Get Your Ideas?* by Sandy Asher (New York: Walker, 1987), 16–19.

27. "MASL 1991 Mark Twain Award Interview with Lois Lowry." (St. Louis: Missouri Association of School Librarians, 1991, videotape).

28. Lois Lowry, "Newbery Medal Acceptance," *Horn Book* 66 (1990): 416; hereafter cited in text as "Newbery 1990."

29. Lois Lowry, *"Number the Stars:* Lois Lowry's Journey to the Newbery Award," *Reading Teacher* 44 (1990): 99; hereafter cited in text as "Journey."

30. In 1997 E. L. Konigsburg became the fifth writer to win the Newbery Award twice.

31. Lois Lowry, " 'Face-to-face' with Lois Lowry," *Follett Forum* (Spring 1989): 1.

32. Nancy Gilson, "Absolutely Lowry: Award-Winning Children's Author Captures Humor, Seriousness of Growing Up," *Columbus Dispatch,* February 8, 1996, 6E.

33. Walter Lorraine, "Lois Lowry," *Horn Book* 70 (1994): 426.

Chapter Two

1. Lois Lowry, *A Summer to Die* (Boston: Houghton, 1977), 3.

2. Letter to Lois Lowry from Melanie Kroupa, September 14, 1976.

3. Lois Lowry, Manuscript materials for *A Summer to Die,* Kerlan Collection, Children's Literature Research Library, University of Minnesota.

4.   Mary M. Burns, "A Summer to Die," *Horn Book* 53 (August 1977): 451; Mary Hobbs, "A Summer to Die," *Junior Bookshelf* 43 (August 1979): 224–25.

5.   Linda R. Silver, "A Summer to Die," *School Library Journal* (May 1977): 63.

6.   Jeanne Bracken and Sharon Wigutoff, *Books for Today's Readers: An Annotated Bibliography of Recommended Fiction for Ages 10–14* (New York: Feminist Press, 1981), 7.

7.   Lois Lowry, *Find a Stranger, Say Good-Bye* (Boston: Houghton, 1978), 12; hereafter cited in text as *Stranger*.

8.   See Joseph Campbell, *The Hero with a Thousand Faces* (New York: Pantheon, 1949).

9.   Lois Lowry, Manuscript materials for *Find a Stranger, Say Goodbye*, Kerlan Collection, Children's Literature Research Library, University of Minnesota. The Kerlan Collection's typescript of *Find a Stranger, Say Goodbye* reveals that the novel was originally titled *Goodbye, Green Panther*.

10.   Marjorie Lewis, "Find a Stranger, Say Goodbye," *School Library Journal* (May 1978): 77–78; David Rees, "Find a Stranger, Say Goodbye," *Times Literary Supplement,* March 28, 1980, 356; Ethel Heins, *Horn Book* 54 (June 1978): 258.

11.   Lance Salway, "Find a Stranger, Say Goodbye," *Signal* 32 (1980): 121.

12.   G. Robert Carlsen, Elizabeth A. Belden, and Anne S. Harker, "1979 Books for Young Adults Book Poll," *English Journal* (December 1979): 78–79.

13.   In October 1994, children's novelist, Patricia Hermes, author of children's novels such as *Mama Let's Dance* (1991) and *Take Care of My Girl* (1992), told me how much she liked *Autumn Street* and that she felt it should have won the Newbery Prize.

14.   Quite appropriately, according to the manuscript materials in the Kerlan Collection, Lowry had originally planned to call the novel *At the End of Autumn*.

15.   Lois Lowry, *Autumn Street* (Boston: Houghton, 1980); hereafter cited in text as *Autumn*.

16.   Constance C. Greene, *New York Times Book Review* (August 17, 1980): 18; Greene is the author of *Philip Hall Likes Me, I Reckon Maybe* (1974).

17.   Marilyn Singer, *School Library Journal* (April 1980): 125–26.

18.   Faith McNulty, *New Yorker* (December 1, 1980): 222.

19.   Barbara Elleman, *Booklist* 76 (1980): 1206; Paul Heins, *Horn Book* 56 (1980): 409.

Chapter Three

1.   See Mary M. Burns, "Anastasia Again!," *Horn Book* 57 (1981): 335–36; and Eric Kimmel, "Anastasia Agonistes: The Tragicomedy of Lois Lowry," *Horn Book* 63 (1987): 84; hereafter cited in text.

2.   The students' humorous responses to Wordsworth's poem, Lowry explains, were written with the help of her daughter, Alix, who was attending Vassar at the time (Chaston 1994).

3.   Ann A. Flowers, "Anastasia Krupnik," *Horn Book* 55 (1979): 663.

4.   Barbara Elleman, "Anastasia Krupnik," *Booklist* 76 (October 15, 1979): 354. See also Brad Owens, "10 Years Old and Growing," *The Christian Science Monitor,* January 14, 1980, B6.

5.   Lois Lowry, *Anastasia Again!* (Boston: Houghton, 1981), 4; hereafter cited in text as *Again.*

6.   For a further discussion of nineteenth-century versions of this sort of character, see Joel D. Chaston, "The Quixotic Reader in Nineteenth-Century British Fiction" (Ph.D. diss., University of Utah, 1989).

7.   See Joel D. Chaston, "Polistopolis and Torquilstone: Nesbit, Eager, and the Question of Imitation," *Lion and the Unicorn: A Critical Journal of Children's Literature* 17 (1993): 73-82.

8.   Judith St. George, "Anastasia Again!," *New York Times Book Review,* February 28, 1982, 31.

9.   See Zena Sutherland, "Anastasia Again!," *Bulletin of the Center for Children's Books* 35.5 (January 1982): 90; Marilyn Kaye, "Anastasia Again!," *School Library Journal* (October 1981): 144; and Joseph B. Browne, "Anastasia Again!," *Catholic Library World* 53 (1982): 356.

10.   Lois Lowry, *Anastasia at Your Service* (Boston: Houghton, 1982), 3.

11.   Lois Lowry, Manuscript materials for *Anastasia at Your Service,* Kerlan Collection, Children's Literature Research Library, University of Minnesota. According to manuscript materials in the children's literature research collection at the University of Minnesota, "Anastasia Atcher Service" was also the novel's original title.

12.   Zena Sutherland, "Anastasia at Your Service," *Bulletin of the Center for Children's Books* 36 (December 1982): 72.

13.   Ann A. Flowers, "Anastasia at Your Service," *Horn Book* 58 (1982): 650.

14.   Ruth M. Stein, "Anastasia at Your Service," *Language Arts* 60 (1983): 360.

15.   Lois Lowry, *Anastasia, Ask Your Analyst* (Boston: Houghton, 1984); hereafter cited in the text as *Analyst.*

16.   Kate M. Flanagan, "Anastasia, Ask Your Analyst," *Horn Book* 60 (1984): 330.

17.   Carolyn Noah, "Anastasia, Ask Your Analyst," *School Library Journal* (May 1984): 82.

18.   See Peter Christen Asbjornsen, *Popular Tales from the Norse,* tr. G. W. Dasent (New York: Putnam's, 1908).

19.   Louisa May Alcott, *Little Women* (1868–69; reprint, New York: Penguin, 1989), 117.

20.   Lois Lowry, *Anastasia on Her Own* (Boston: Houghton, 1985), 131.

21.   See "Anastasia on Her Own," *Bulletin of the Center for Children's Books* 38 (May 1985): 170; Ann A. Flowers, "Anastasia on Her Own," *Horn Book* 61 (1985): 556; and Zaidman, 259.

Chapter Four

1.   See Robert Havinghurst's *Developmental Tasks and Education* (New York: McKay, 1972).

2.   Lois Lowry, *Anastasia Has the Answers* (Boston: Houghton, 1986), 18–19; hereafter cited in text as *Answers*.

3.   Lois Lowry, "Remembering Pennsylvania," in *Literacy through Literature: Proceedings of the 38th Annual Conference and Course on Literacy, June 1991,* ed. Saundra Koebler, Stephen A. Kirsch, and Rita M. Bean (Pittsburgh: University of Pittsburgh, 1991), 17; hereafter cited in text as "Pennsylvania."

4.   Zena Sutherland, "Anastasia Has the Answers," *Bulletin of the Center for Children's Books* 39 (May 1986): 173.

5.   Lois Lowry, *Anastasia's Chosen Career* (Boston: Houghton, 1987), 33; hereafter cited in text as *Career*.

6.   See Aileen Pace Nilsen and Kenneth Donelson, *Literature for Today's Young Adults,* 4th ed. (New York: Harper, 1993), 143.

7.   Dudley B. Carlson, "Anastasia's Chosen Career," *School Library Journal* (September 1987): 180.

8.   Lois Lowry, *All about Sam* (Boston: Houghton, 1988), 5; hereafter cited in text as *Sam*.

9.   Ann A. Flowers, "All about Sam," *Horn Book* 65 (1989): 72.

10.   Trev Jones, "All about Sam," *School Library Journal* (August 1988): 96.

11.   Lois Lowry, *Anastasia at This Address* (Boston: Houghton, 1991): 6; hereafter cited in text as *Address*.

12.   See Zena Sutherland, "Anastasia at This Address," *Bulletin of the Center for Children's Books* 44 (March 1991): 169; and Diane Roback, "Anastasia at This Address," *Publishers Weekly* (January 27, 1992): 58.

13.   Lois Lowry, *Attaboy, Sam!* (Boston: Houghton, 1992), 5; hereafter cited in text as *Attaboy*.

14.   Hazel Rochman, "Attaboy, Sam!," *Booklist* 88 (February 15, 1992): 1106.

15.   Roger Sutton, "Attaboy, Sam!," *Bulletin of the Center for Children's Books* 45 (April 1992): 213.

16.   Lois Lowry, *Anastasia, Absolutely* (Boston: Houghton, 1995), 29; hereafter cited in text as *Absolutely*.

17.   "Anastasia, Absolutely," *Kirkus Reviews* (October 1, 1995).

18.   Maeve Visser Knoth, "Anastasia, Absolutely," *Horn Book* 71 (1995): 761.

19. Michael Cart, "Anastasia, Absolutely," *New York Times,* January 14, 1996, sec. 7, p. 23.

20. Lois Lowry, *See You Around, Sam!* (Boston: Houghton, 1996), 51; hereafter cited in text as *Around.*

21. Roger Sutton, "See You Around, Sam!" *Horn Book* 72 (1996): 597.

22. Michael Cart, *What's So Funny?: Wit and Humor in American Children's Literature* (New York: HarperCollins, 1995), 193.

Chapter Five

1. Lois Lowry, *The One Hundredth Thing about Caroline* (Boston: Houghton, 1983), 6.

2. Incidentally, writing the scenes set in the museum prompted Lowry to take a quick trip to New York City with one of her sons to spend a day in the real Museum of Natural History.

3. Zena Sutherland, "The One Hundredth Thing about Caroline," *Bulletin of the Center for Children's Books* 37 (February 1984): 112.

4. Ethel Heins, "The One Hundredth Thing about Caroline," *Horn Book* 59 (1983): 711.

5. Kathleen Brachmann, "The One Hundredth Thing about Caroline," *School Library Journal* (October 1983): 160.

6. Lois Lowry, *Taking Care of Terrific* (Boston: Houghton, 1983), 7.

7. Lois Lowry, "Introduction," in *The Secret Garden* by Francis Hodgson Burnett (1911; reprint, New York: Bantam, 1987), viii; hereafter cited in text as "Garden."

8. "Taking Care of Terrific," *Kirkus Reviews* 51 (March 15, 1983): 310.

9. Zena Sutherland, "Taking Care of Terrific," *Bulletin of the Center for Children's Books* 36 (March 15, 1983): 129.

10. Karen Jameyson, "Taking Care of Terrific," *Horn Book* 59 (1983): 129.

11. Lois Lowry, *Us and Uncle Fraud* (Boston: Houghton, 1984), 23.

12. Ethel R. Twichell, "Us and Uncle Fraud," *Horn Book* 60 (1984): 759.

13. Zena Sutherland, *"Bulletin of the Center for Children's Books* 38 (December 1984): 71.

14. Lyn Littlefield Hoopes, *Christian Science Monitor,* March 1, 1985, B5.

15. Lois Lowry, *Switcharound* (Boston: Houghton, 1985), 6.

16. "Switcharound," *Bulletin of the Center for Children's Books* 39 (January 1980): 90.

17. Kristiana Gregory, *Los Angeles Times Book Review,* February 16, 1986, 9.

18. Ilene Cooper, "Your Move, J. P.!," *Booklist* 86 (March 1, 1990): 1345.

19. Ruth Ann Smith, *Bulletin of the Center for Children's Books* 43 (March 1990): 169.

20. Lois Lowry, *Your Move, J. P.!* (Boston: Houghton, 1990), 5; hereafter cited in text as *Move*.

21. Ethel R. Twichell, "Your Move, J. P.!" *Horn Book* 66 (1990): 201.

22. Lois Lowry, "Splendor," in *Short Takes: A Short Story Collection for Young Readers,* ed. Elizabeth Segel (New York: Lothrop, 1986), 86; hereafter cited in text as "Splendor."

23. Lois Lowry, "The Harringtons' Daughter," in *A Gathering of Flowers: Stories about Being Young in America* (New York: Harper, 1990), 32; hereafter cited in text as "Daughter."

24. Lois Lowry, "The Tree House," in *The Big Book of Peace,* ed. Ann Durell and Marilyn Sachs and illus. Trina Schart Hyman (New York: Dutton, 1990), 31; hereafter cited in text as "Tree House."

25. "Elliot's House," in *The Big Book of the Planet,* ed. Ann Durrell, Jean Craighead George, and Katherine Paterson (New York: Dutton, 1993), 117; hereafter cited in text as "Elliot's."

26. Lois Lowry, "Holding," in *Am I Blue?: Coming Out from the Silence,* ed. Marion Dane Bauer (New York: Harper, 1994), 184–85.

27. Marion Dane Bauer, "Introduction," in *Am I Blue?: Coming Out of the Silence,* ed. Bauer, xi.

Chapter Six

1. Anita Silvey, "Editorial: The Giver," *Horn Book* 69 (1993): 392.

2. Lois Lowry, *Number the Stars* (Boston: Houghton, 1989), 24; hereafter cited in text as *Number*.

3. Ann A. Flowers, "Rabble Starkey," *Horn Book* 63 (1987): 463.

4. Lois Lowry, *"Rabble Starkey:* A Voice from a Surprising Place," in *The Voice of the Narrator in Children's Literature: Insights from Writers and Critics,* ed. Charlotte Otten and Gary D. Schmidt (New York: Greenwood, 1989); hereafter cited in text as "Voice."

5. Lois Lowry, *Rabble Starkey* (Boston: Houghton, 1987), 6; hereafter cited in text as *Rabble*.

6. Lois Lowry, "Calling It Quits," *The Writer* (April 1989): 14.

7. Lois Lowry, Manuscript materials for *Rabble Starkey,* Kerlan Collection, Children's Literature Research Library, University of Minnesota.

8. Lou Ann Walker, "She Didn't Tell on Norman," *New York Times Book Review,* May 17, 1987, 33.

9. Betsy Hearne, "Rabble Starkey," *Bulletin of the Center for Children's Books* 40 (March 1987): 130.

10. Kathleen Brachmann, "Rabble Starkey," *School Library Journal* (April 1987): 99.

11. Letters from Lois Lowry to Walter Lorraine, September 11, 1988 and September 22, 1988, in manuscript materials for *Number the Stars,* Kerlan Collection, Children's Literature Research Library, University of Minnesota.

12. Mary M. Burns, "Number the Stars," *Horn Book* 63 (1989): 371.

13. Denise Wilms, "Number the Stars," *Booklist* 85 (March 1, 1989): 1194.

14. Edith Milton, "Escape from Copenhagen," *New York Times Book Review,* May 21, 1989, 32.

15. Lois Lowry, Manuscript materials for *The Giver,* Kerlan Collection, Children's Literature Research Library, University of Minnesota; hereafter cited in text as "Giver Manuscript."

16. Lois Lowry, *The Giver* (Boston: Houghton, 1993), 63.

17. Karen Ray, "The Giver," *New York Times Book Review,* October 31, 1993, 26.

18. Jorge Luis Borges, "Funes, the Memorious," in his *Personal Anthology,* ed. Anthony Kerrigan and tr. Anthony Kerrigan (New York: Grove Press, 1967), 35–43.

19. Ursula K. Le Guin, "The Ones Who Walk Away from Omelas," in *The Wind's Twelve Quarters* (New York: Harper, 1975), 282.

20. See "The Giver," *Publisher's Weekly* (February 15, 1993): 240. Despite this claim, when I asked Lowry about "The Little Match Girl," she could not remember how the story ended.

21. Ann A. Flowers, "The Giver," *Horn Book* 69 (1993): 458.

22. Patty Campbell, "The Sand in the Oyster," *Horn Book* 69 (1993): 716–21.

Chapter Seven

1. See *New York Times,* 22May 22, 1995.

2. "Publisher's Weekly Children's Bestsellers: July 1975," *Publisher's Weekly* (July 17, 1995): 207.

3. Ian Ith, "Neighborhood Play Stages Holocaust Play," *News Tribune,* August 3, 1994, B7.

4. Nancy Maes, "Shining Lesson: 'Number the Stars' Recalls the Holocaust," *Chicago Tribune,* October 19, 1995, "Tempo" section, 2.

5. Joel D. Chaston, "American Children's Fiction of the Eighties: Continuity and Innovation," *Children's Literature in Education* 22 (1991): 299.

6. These papers included Adrienne Kertzer's "A Mother Steps out of the Pattern," Margaret Cook's "On a Bicycle to Elsewhere: Childlore from *The Giver,*" Virginia A. Walter's "Metaphor and Mantra: The Functions of Story in *Number the Stars,*" and Laura M. Zaidman's "*Number the Stars:* A Post-Holocaust 'Little Red-Riding Hood.' "

7. Paula Cowan, "Initiatives Help Allay Spielberg's Fears," *The Herald* (Glasgow), May 10, 1994, 2.

8. Dave and Danna Pedry, "Guest Column: Blume, Lowry Novels as Corrupt as *Playboy,*" *Star-Tribune* (Casper, Wyoming), January 29, 1985, A15.

9. Janus Adams, "Children's Buyer Beware," *Ms.* 5.2 (September/October 1994): 72–74.

10. Sharon French, "Letter to the Editor," *Indianapolis Star,* September 16, 1995, A13.

11. Karla Fultz, "Letter to the Editor," *Indianapolis Star,* September 26, 1995, A11.

12. Susie Johnson, "Letter to the Editor," *Indianapolis News,* September 28, 1995, A11.

Selected Bibliography

PRIMARY WORKS

Novels

Stay!: Keeper's Tale. Boston: Houghton, 1997.
See You Around, Sam! Boston: Houghton, 1996.
Anastasia, Absolutely. Boston: Houghton, 1995.
The Giver. Boston: Houghton, 1993; New York: Dell, 1994.
Attaboy, Sam! Illus. Diane de Groat. Boston: Houghton, 1992.
Anastasia at This Address. Boston: Houghton, 1991.
Your Move, J. P.! Boston: Houghton, 1990; New York: Dell, 1991.
Number the Stars. Boston: Houghton, 1989; New York: Dell, 1990.
All about Sam. Illus. Diane de Groat. Boston: Houghton, 1988; New York: Dell, 1989.
Anastasia's Chosen Career. Boston: Houghton, 1987; New York: Dell, 1988.
Rabble Starkey. Boston: Houghton, 1987; New York: Dell, 1988.
Anastasia Has the Answers. Boston: Houghton, 1986; New York: Dell, 1987.
Anastasia on Her Own. Boston: Houghton, 1985; New York: Dell, 1986.
Switcharound. Boston: Houghton, 1985; New York: Dell, 1987.
Anastasia, Ask Your Analyst. Boston: Houghton, 1984; New York: Dell, 1985.
Us and Uncle Fraud. Boston: Houghton, 1984; New York: Dell, 1985.
Taking Care of Terrific. Boston: Houghton, 1983; New York: Dell, 1984.
The One Hundredth Thing about Caroline. Boston: Houghton, 1983; New York: Dell, 1985.
Anastasia at Your Service. Boston: Houghton, 1982; New York: Dell, 1984.
Anastasia Again! Boston: Houghton, 1981; New York: Dell, 1982.
Autumn Street. Boston: Houghton, 1980; New York: Dell, 1982.
Anastasia Krupnik. Boston: Houghton, 1979; New York: Bantam, 1981.
Find a Stranger, Say Good-Bye. Boston: Houghton, 1978; New York: Pocket, 1979; New York: Dell, 1990.
A Summer to Die. Boston: Houghton, 1977; New York: Bantam, 1979.

Short Fiction

"Holding." In *Am I Blue?: Coming Out from the Silence,* ed. Marion Dane Bauer. New York: HarperCollins, 1994. 177–89.

"Elliot's House." In *The Big Book for Our Planet,* ed. Ann Durrell, Jean Craig-head George, and Katherine Paterson. New York: Dutton, 1993. 116–21.

"The Harrington's Daughter." In *A Gathering of Flowers: Stories about Being Young in America,* ed. Joyce Carol Thomas. New York: Harper, 1990. 23–34.

"The Tree House." In *The Big Book for Peace,* ed. Ann Durrell and Marilyn Sachs. New York: Dutton, 1990. 30–38.

"Splendor." In *Short Takes: A Short Story Collection for Young Readers,* ed. Elizabeth Segel. Illus. Joseph A. Smith. New York: Lothrop, 1986. 84–105.

"Crow Call." *Redbook* (December 1975): 38–39.

Nonfiction—Textbooks

Editor. *Literature of the American Revolutionary Period.* Portland, Maine: Walch, 1975.

Editor. *Black American Literature.* Portland, Maine: Walch, 1974.

Nonfiction—Educational Pamphlets and Photography

A Teenage Pregnancy. Portland, Maine: Walch, 1980. Slides.

Buying a House. Portland, Maine: Walch, 1979. Slides.

Here at Kennebunkport. Text by Frederick H. Lewis. New York: Durell, 1978. Photographs.

Personal Values. Portland, Maine: Walch, 1978. Illustrated pamphlet.

A Day in the Life of a Waitress. Portland, Maine: Walch, 1977. Slides.

Shoplifting. Portland, Maine: Walch, 1977. Slides.

Values and the Family. Portland, Maine: Walch, 1977. Illustrated pamphlet.

Slides on Thoreau. Portland, Maine: Walch, 1976. Slides.

Nonfiction—Feature Articles in Newspapers and Magazines

"Traveling Down East: Ogunquit in June." *Down East* 25 (June 1979): 31–34.

"Tarzan of the Maine Woods." *Down East* 26 (September 1979): 70–75.

"Good News from the Countryside." *Down East* 24 (March 1978): 39–41, 58.

"Traveling Down East: Kennebunkport." *Down East* 24 (May 1978): 21–22, 24.

"Sold! To the Young Couple with the Big Ideas: F. O. Bailey, Maine's Oldest Auction House." *Down East* 24 (July 1978): 56–61.

"A Passion for Victoriana." *Down East* 25 (September 1978): 58–63.

"Thanksgiving in Wyeth Country." *Down East* 25 (November 1978): 19–20, 23–24, 27–28.

"I Could Be a Rabbit Forever—Children's Theatre of Main." *Down East* 23 (March 1977): 36–39.

"Finding Nova Scotia's Heartbeat." *New York Times* (April 24, 1977), sec. 10, p. 9.

"Hollywood on the Kennebec." *Down East* 23 (May 1977): 44–49, 69–70.

"Windjammer Cook." *Down East* 23 (June 1977): 80–81, 96.

"Learning to See." *Down East* 24 (August 1977): 48–53.

"The Gang that Couldn't Shoot Straight." *Down East* 24 (October 1977): 47–51.

"King of the Occult." *Down East* 24 (November 1977): 39–41, 61.

"The Recital." *Philadelphia* 68 (December 1977): 118.

"Saint Patrick's at Newcastle." *Down East* 24 (December 1977): 14–20.

"The Maine Boyhoods of Longfellow and Hawthorne." *Down East* 22 (March 1976): 32–35, 58.

"The Old Port Exchange." *Down East* 22 (June 1976): 50–55.

"The Berdans of Antiques Row." *Down East* 23 (July 1976): 56–59.

"The Colonial Life at Strawberry Banke." *New York Times* (September 12, 1976), sec. 10, p. 7.

"New Life for the House Captain Lord Built." *Down East* 23 (November 1976): 32–37.

"Eastport, Maine: The Same Salty Whiff." *Yankee* 39 (May 1975): 66–71.

"Where F. D. R. Sunned." *New York Times* (June 1, 1975), sec. XX, pp. 1, 18.

"Picturing Children as They Really Are." *New York Times* (December 14, 1975), sec. II, pp. 44–45.

"How Does It Feel to Be on a TV Quiz Show? Don't Ask." *New York Times* (March 31, 1974) sec. 2, pp. 1, 23.

Nonfiction—Literary Articles, Reviews, and Speeches

"Introduction." In *Dear Author: Students Write about Books That Changed Their Lives*, collected by *Weekly Reader's Read Magazine*. Berkeley, Calif.: Conari Press, 1995. ix–xii.

"Voices of the Creators: Lois Lowry." In *Children's Books and Their Creators*. Ed. Anita Silvey. Boston: Houghton, 1995. 420.

"Newbery Medal Acceptance." *Horn Book* 70 (1994): 414–22.

"On Writing *The Giver*." *Book Links* (May 1994): 11.

"Lois Lowry." In *Speaking for Ourselves, Too: More Autobiographical Sketches by Notable Authors of Books for Young Adults*. Ed. Donald Gallo. Urbana, Ill.: NCTE, 1993. 125–27.

"Remembering Pennsylvania." In *Literacy through Literature. Proceedings of the Annual Conference and Course on Literacy* (38th, Pittsburgh, Pennsylvania). Ed. Saundra Koebler, Stephen A. Kirsch, and Rita M. Bean. University of Pittsburgh, 1991. 15–20. ERIC microfiche ED437503.

"Newbery Medal Acceptance." *Horn Book* 66 (1990): 412–21.

"*Number the Stars*: Lois Lowry's Journey to the Newbery Award." *Reading Teacher* 44 (1990): 98–101.

"Trusting the Reader." *Writer* (May 1990): 7–8.

"Calling It Quits." *Writer* (April 1989): 13–14, 47.

"Rabble Starkey: A Voice from a Surprising Place." In *The Voice of the Narrator in Children's Literature: Insights from Writers and Critics*. Ed. Charlotte Otten and Gary D. Schmidt. New York: Greenwood, 1989. 180–83.

"Acceptance Speech for the 1987 Boston Globe-Horn Book Award for Fiction." *Horn Book* 64 (1988): 29–31.

"Introduction." In *The Secret Garden* by Francis Hodgson Burnett. 1911. Reprint, New York: Dell, 1987.

"Remembering How It Was." *Writer* (July 1987): 16–19.

"Stories behind Stories." In *Where Do You Get Your Ideas?* by Sandy Asher. New York: Walker, 1987. 11–13.

"Afterword." In *Pollyanna* by Eleanor H. Porter. 1913. Reprint, New York: Dell, 1986. 219–20.

"Lois Lowry." In *Something about the Author Autobiography Series*. Vol. 3. Ed. Adele Sarkissian. Detroit: Gale, 1986. 131–46.

"Two Teen-agers with Ailing Grandparents in the Family." *Los Angeles Times* (November 15, 1986), pt. 5, p. 5

Audiovisual Adaptations

"Anastasia Krupnik." (Filmstrip adaptation of Lowry's *Anastasia Krupnik*). Englewood, Colo.: Cheshire Corporation, 1987.

"Taking Care of Terrific." Writ. Kenneth Cavander (Television motion picture adaptation of *Taking Care of Terrific* by Lowry). Dir. Jim Purdy. *Wonderworks*. Starring Joanne Vannicola and Mario Van Peebles. PBS. January 16, 1987. WETA-TV and Paragon Motion Pictures.

"I Don't Know Who I Am." Writ. Daryl Warner and Carolyn H. Miller (Television motion picture adaptation of *Find a Stranger, Say Goodbye* by Lowry). Dir. Joe Manduke. Starring Susan Meyers. *NBC Special Treats*. Prod. Joanne A. Curley. November 20, 1979. Daniel Wilson Productions.

SECONDARY WORKS

Interviews

Cary, Alice. "And They All Lived . . . Ever After." *Boston Sunday Herald, Sunday People,* June 26, 1994, 1, 5–7. A detailed photo-essay based on a personal interview after Lowry received her second Newbery Award.

Chaston, Joel D. Personal interview with Lois Lowry. October 6, 1994, at her home in Cambridge, Massachusetts.

"Face to Face with Lois Lowry." *Follett Forum* (Spring 1989): 1–3. An interview including a discussion of Lowry's writing process.

Gilson, Nancy. "Absolutely Lowry: Award-Winning Children's Author Captures Humor, Seriousness of Growing Up." *Columbus Dispatch,* February 8,

1996. This article, written at the time Lowry published *Anastasia, Absolutely*, includes comments on the death of Lowry's son, the creation of Anastasia Krupnik, and her receipt of the Newbery Medal for *The Giver*.

Hendershot, Judy, and Jackie Peck. "An Interview with Lois Lowry, 1994 Newbery Medal Winner." *Reading Teacher* 48 (December 1994–January 1995). 308–9. A brief interview focusing primarily on Lowry's creation of *The Giver* and the novel's possible classroom uses.

"Lois Lowry." Morristown, Pa.: J. S. Weiss, 1990. A profile of and interview with Lowry. Videotape.

Lorraine, Walter. "Lois Lowry: Author Study Tape." Holmes, Pa.: Trumpet Club, 1994. An interview intended for young readers with an emphasis on *The Giver*. Audiocassette.

"MASL 1991 Mark Twain Award Interview with Lois Lowry." St. Louis: Missouri Association of School Librarians, 1991. Conducted by a child, this interview took place when Lowry accepted the Mark Twain Award for *All About Sam*. Videotape.

Mehren, Elizabeth. "Author Lois Lowry Never Planned to Write Fiction for Adults, but Fate and a Natural Connection to Her Audience Stepped In." *Los Angeles Times*, "Life and Style," November 9, 1994, 3. An article, prompted by Lowry's receipt of two Newbery Prizes, focusing on her decision to write for children.

Miller, Dieter. "Lois Lowry." In *Authors and Artists for Young People,* vol. 5. Ed. Agnes Garrett and Helga P. McCue. Detroit: Gale, 1990. 129–40. An article piecing together information from several interviews, including new material gathered by Miller.

Nicholson, George. "Lois Lowry: Authors on Tape." Holmes, Pa.: Trumpet Club, 1990. This interview is a good introduction to Lowry's life and includes discussion of the Anastasia books and *Autumn Street*. Audiocassette.

Pearlman, Mickey, ed. "Lois Lowry" in her *Listen to Their Voices: Twenty Interviews with Women Who Write*. New York: Norton, 1993. 172–82. Pearlman's interview is woven into an essay about Lowry that includes discussion of her divorce and the writing of *Number the Stars*.

Ross, Jean. "Lois Lowry." *Contemporary Authors*. New Revision Series, vol. 13. Detroit: Gale, 1984. 333–36. A relatively early interview, frequently cited by other writers. It treats Lowry's writing process and the creation of the character Anastasia Krupnik.

Smith, Amanda. *"Publisher's Weekly* Interviews: Lois Lowry." *Publishers Weekly* 229 (February 21, 1986): 152–53. An interview that includes discussion of Lowry's early life and her attitudes toward writing. The photograph in this interview has appeared on the book jackets of many books by Lowry.

"A Visit With Lois Lowry." Boston: Houghton, 1985. A visit with Lowry in her New Hampshire farmhouse, in which she talks about some of her books and her writing process. Videotape.

Books and Parts of Books

Allen, Janet S. "Exploring the Individual's Responsibility in Society in *The Giver* and *Brave New World*." In *Adolescent Literature as a Complement to the Classics,* vol. II. Ed. Joan F. Kaywell. Norwood, Mass.: Christopher-Gordon, 1995. 199–212. This article explores *The Giver* as a dystopian novel, as well as its similarities to Aldous Huxley's *Brave New World*, in the context of a teaching unit.

Cart, Michael. *What's So Funny? Wit and Humor in American Children's Literature.* New York: HarperCollins, 1995. Cart concludes a discussion of domestic humor in American children's literature by addressing the Anastasia series, in particular *Anastasia Krupnik* and *Anastasia Has the Answers.*

Chaston, Joel. *A Literature Guide to Lois Lowry's Number the Stars.* Cambridge, Mass.: Bookwise, 1993. This guide contains an introductory essay and a close analysis of individual chapters, in question-and-answer format, along with suggestions for teaching the novel.

————. "The Giver." In *Beacham's Guide to Young Adult Literature,* vol. 6. Ed. Kirk Beetz. Washington, D.C.: Beacham, 1994. 3255–63. An analysis of the themes, characters, and literary qualities of *The Giver,* along with topics for student discussion.

Commire, Anne, ed. "Lois Lowry." *Something about the Author.* Detroit: Gale, 1981. 120–22. A biographical and bibliographical essay containing comments by Lowry herself.

Cullinan, Bernice. "Profile: Lois Lowry." In *Literature and the Child,* 2d ed. San Diego: Harcourt, 1989. 406–7. A biographical sketch that recounts the events described in "The Recital."

Markham, Lois. *Lois Lowry.* Santa Barbara: Learning Works, 1995. A general, mostly undocumented, biography intended for young readers with material drawn largely from Lowry's essay in *Something about the Author, Autobiographical Series* and an apparent interview.

Norton, Donna E. *Through the Eyes of a Child: An Introduction to Children's Literature,* 3rd ed. New York: Macmillan, 1991. Includes brief discussions of *Number the Stars*, *Anastasia on Her Own*, and *Anastasia Krupnik.*

Sutherland, Zena, and May Hill Arbuthnot. "Lois Lowry: *A Summer to Die*, the *Anastasia Krupnik* Books, *Rabble Starkey*, and *Autumn Street*." In *Children and Books,* 8th ed. Glenview, Ill.: Scott, Foresman, 1991. 365. A brief review of several of Lowry's books.

Zaidman, Laura. "Lois Lowry." In *Dictionary of Literary Biography: American Writers for Children Since 1960—Fiction,* vol. 52. Ed. Glenn E. Estes. Detroit: Gale, 1986. 249–61. A detailed overview of Lowry's life and a discussion of her works through 1986.

————. "Lois Lowry." In *Twentieth-Century Young Adult Writers,* ed. Laura Standley Berger. Detroit: St. James Press, 1994. 408–410. A brief overview of Lowry's career as a writer.

Articles

Adams, Janus. "Children's Books: Buyer Beware," *Ms.* 5 (September/October 1994): 72–74. Based on a misreading of the text, this article criticizes *The Giver* as racist and sexist.

Apseloff, Marily Fain. "Lois Lowry: Facing the Censors." *Para•doxa: Studies in World Literary Genres* 2.3–4 (1996): 480–85.

Campbell, Patty. "Sand in the Oyster." *Horn Book* 69 (November/December 1993): 717–21. Campbell discusses *The Giver* and David Skinner's *You Must Kiss a Whale* (1994) as extraordinary works that are daring in their complexity and challenging in their ambiguity. According to Campbell, *The Giver* draws from three of the common ways for dystopian novels to end.

Cart, Michael. "Anastasia, Absolutely." *New York Times,* January 14, 1996, sec. 7, p. 23. In this review of *Anastasia, Absolutely,* Cart takes the opportunity to discuss the Anastasia series as a whole.

Chaston, Joel D. "American Children's Fiction of the Eighties: Continuity and Innovation." *Children's Literature in Education* 22 (1991): 223–32. A section of this article discusses well-known children's fiction writers who have taken risks during the 1980s and focuses on Lowry's *Number the Stars* and *Rabble Starkey*.

———. "The Writing Teacher in Contemporary Children's Fiction." *Language Arts Journal of Michigan* 5.3 (1990): 1–8. A discussion of writing teachers in three children's novels, including Lowry's *Anastasia Krupnik*, Beverly Cleary's *Dear Mr. Henshaw* (1983), and Paula Danziger's *The Cat Ate My Gymsuit* (1974).

Corsaro, Julie. "The Inside Story: Lois Lowry's *The Giver*." *Book Links* (May 1994): 9–10. A summary of the novel, followed by an introduction to dystopian literature and suggested discussion questions.

Dobson, Dorothy. "Getting a Grip on World War II: Using a Novel to Introduce the Topic." *The Instructor* 104 (March 1994): 40. Specific guidelines for using *Number the Stars* to introduce a teaching unit on Holocaust literature.

Haley-James, Shirley. "Lois Lowry." *Horn Book* 64 (1990): 422–23. A biographical sketch by a good friend of Lowry's on the occasion of Lowry's first Newbery award.

Kertzer, Adrienne. "Reclaiming Her Maternal Pre-Text: Little Red Riding Hood's Mother and Three Young Adult Novels." A close reading of Lowry's *Find a Stranger, Say Goodbye,* Gillian Cross's *Wolf* (1990), and Jean Thesman's *The Rain Catchers* (1991), works that feature adopted daughters searching for their birth mothers. Kertzer argues that in structuring their novels as daughters' quests for maternal pretexts, Lowry, Cross, and Thesman suggest links between rewritings of "Red Riding Hood" and feminist autobiography.

Kimmel, Eric A. "Anastasia Agonistes: The Tragicomedy of Lois Lowry." *Horn Book* 63 (1987): 181–87. The first serious treatment of Lowry's Anastasia books (covering the first six in the series). Kimmel explores the tragic and comic sides of these novels.

Lorraine, Walter. "Lois Lowry." *Horn Book* 70 (1994): 423–26. Lowry's long-time editor and friend comments on her personality and their relationship at the time Lowry won her second Newbery award.

McMullen, Judith Q. "The Spy and the Poet: Young Girls as Writers in *Harriet the Spy* and *Anastasia Krupnik*." In *The Image of the Child: Proceedings of the 1991 International Conference of the Children's Literature Association,* May 30–June 2, 1991. Ed. Sylvia Patterson Iskander. Battle Creek, Mich.: ChLA, 1991. 200–204. A study of what *Anastasia Krupnik* suggests about the development of young writers.

Marinak, Barbara. "Books in the Classroom: The Holocaust." *Horn Book* 69 (May 1993): 368–73. A discussion of the use of Holocaust literature in the classroom, including Lowry's *Number the Stars*.

Siclen, Bill. "Children's Book Festival: Off to Meet the Literary Wizards." *Providence Journal,* October 21, 1994, 1D. A discussion of Lowry's career drawing from a personal interview.

Silvey, Anita. "Editorial: The Giver." *Horn Book Magazine* 69 (1993): 392. This editorial praises Lowry for taking a risk by writing a remarkable novel, one different from her humorous works in tone and scope.

Walters, Karla. "Pills against Sexual 'Stirrings' in Lowry's *The Giver*." A brief discussion of the "excessively politically correct" society of *The Giver*.

Zaidman, Laura. "Lowry's *Number the Stars:* A Post-Holocaust 'Little Red-Riding Hood.' " *Journal of Children's Literature* 22.1 (Spring 1996): 39–42. An exploration of "Little Red Riding Hood" as a subtext of *Number the Stars*.

Index

The Author

Joel D. Chaston was born in Salt Lake City, Utah, and received his Ph.D. in British and American literature from the University of Utah. He has taught at Western Michigan University and is currently an associate professor of English at Southwest Missouri State University, where he teaches courses in children's and young adult literature. A former member of the board of directors of the International Children's Literature Association, he has published articles on children's literature in a variety of journals and books. He is the author of *A Literature Guide to Lois Lowry's Number the Stars* (Bookwise, 1993) and the coauthor of *Theme Exploration: A Voyage of Discovery* (Heinemann, 1993).

The Editor

Ruth K. MacDonald is college dean for the I Have a Dream Foundation in Hartford, Connecticut. She received her B.A. and M.A. in English from the University of Connecticut, her Ph.D. in English from Rutgers University, and her M.B.A. from the University of Texas at El Paso. She is the author of the volumes on Louisa May Alcott, Beatrix Potter, and Dr. Seuss in Twayne's United States Authors and English Authors Series and of the books *Literature for Children in England and America, 1646–1774* (1982) and *Christian's Children: The Influence of John Bunyan's "Pilgrim's Progress" on American Children's Literature* (1989).